The

Confetti Cakes
COOKBOOK

ATJ

The
Confetti Cakes
COOKBOOK

SPECTACULAR **COOKIES, CAKES,** AND **CUPCAKES**
FROM NEW YORK CITY'S FAMED BAKERY

Elisa Strauss

with CHRISTIE MATHESON

Photographs by Alexandra Rowley

Little, Brown and Company
NEW YORK · BOSTON · LONDON

Little, Brown and Company
Hachette Book Group USA
237 Park Avenue, New York, NY 10169
Visit our Web site at www.HachetteBookGroupUSA.com

All photographs are by Alexandra Rowley except for the portrait on page 8, which is by Rose Callahan.

First Edition: April 2007

Library of Congress Cataloging-in-Publication Data
Strauss, Elisa.
    The confetti cakes cookbook: spectacular cookies, cakes, and cupcakes from New York's famed bakery / Elisa Strauss with Christie Matheson.
        p. cm.
    ISBN-13: 978-0-316-11307-6
    ISBN-10: 0-316-11307-7
    1. Cake decorating. 2. Confetti Cakes (Bakery) I. Matheson, Christie. II. Title.
    TX771.2.S77 2006
    641.8'6539 — dc22   2006015900

Design by Gary Tooth / Empire Design Studio

Printed in China

For my mom and dad,
who have shown continuous support, from delivering cakes
to cutting out gum paste and just giving me a hug
when I need it. Their confidence in me has led me to believe
I can do anything in life. **I love you both so much.**

Contents

Introduction

Nothing makes a celebration special like a beautiful, memorable, one-of-a-kind sweet treat — fantastic cookies that will dazzle your friends; the most adorable cupcakes anyone has ever seen; or an elaborate sculpted cake, created especially for the guest of honor. Yes, *you* can do it.

I have always loved to bake. Since I was a little girl, I can remember learning to bake from my grandmother, and some of my sweetest memories come from her kitchen. After several years working in the fashion industry, I picked up a few cake-decorating books and began playing around in my own kitchen, creating surprising cakes for my friends and family — and even had a request to make one for a celebrity in the fashion world. Those cakes made such a splash that guests at the parties told me I should be making cakes full-time. I went to pastry school to learn the fundamentals of baking so I could make any kind of confection imaginable, and six years ago I started my design studio, Confetti Cakes, on the Upper West Side of New York City.

If you can think of it, we can make it at Confetti Cakes. The only limit is the imagination. We have made cakes that look exactly like wine bottles in crates, animals, a roulette wheel, and a wedding dress. One bride surprised her husband-to-be with a groom's cake that looked just like a billiard table. We even make cakes that appear to be savory foods, such as sushi and a Philly cheesesteak!

Confetti Cakes' creations are known for being stylish, elegant, and modern — never stuffy or fussy. We have made cakes for more magazine photo shoots and television shows than I can count. Our clients include some of the most fashion-savvy celebrities in New York, as well as families and companies from all over the city and the region who adore the innovative, fun, and fabulous look of our designs and the delicious flavor of our cakes and fillings — all made from scratch.

Of course, many of my clients and people who have seen me on television want to know how they can make cakes like this at home. I've assembled here our bakery's greatest hits — and provided you with detailed recipes, instructions, techniques, illustrations, and photos so you can make them in your own kitchen. I have made these pieces dozens of times, so over the course of my career I have learned a lot about what works and what doesn't.

In this book are cookies, cupcakes, mini cakes, and cakes for many occasions. Some are super simple, others are more time-consuming. They all are guaranteed to impress, and to make whoever gets them feel incredibly special.

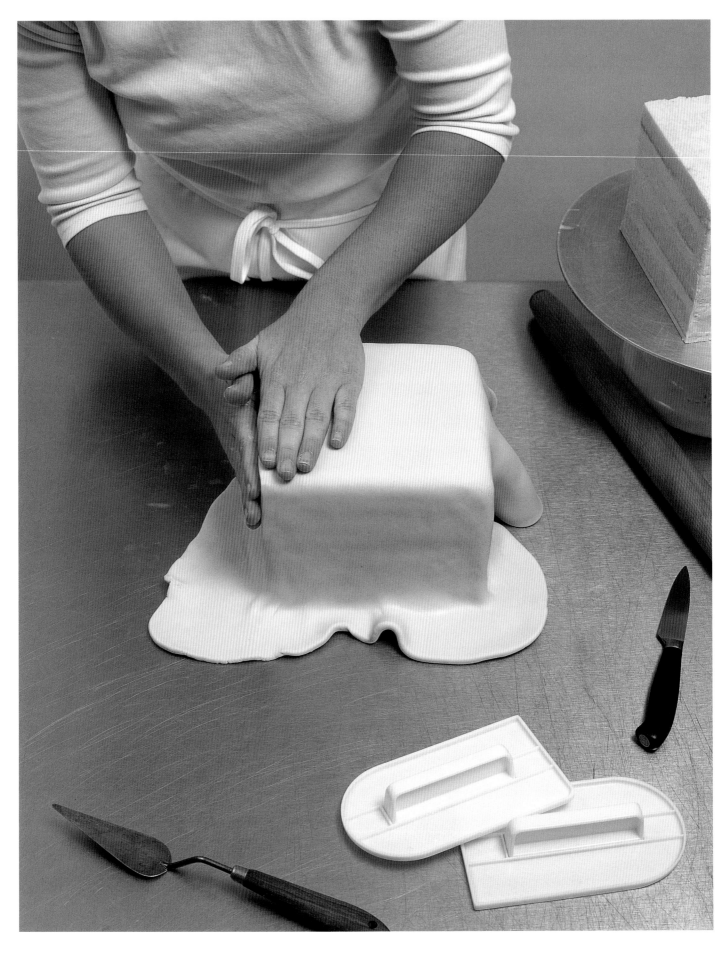

Equipment and Techniques

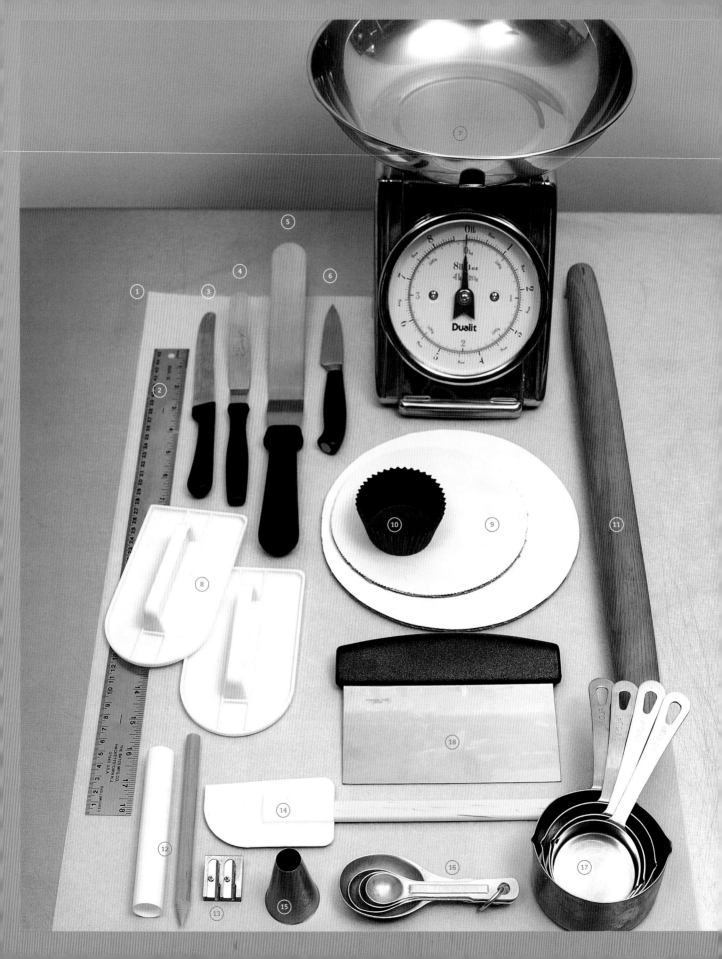

Equipment

I refer to the equipment shown here throughout this book.
Having a good collection of equipment will make
creating great cakes much easier.

1.   PARCHMENT PAPER: This nonstick, oven-safe paper has a variety of uses: lining baking sheets and the bottom of cake pans to keep cookies and cakes from sticking; rolling out cookie dough, between two sheets of it, tracing designs, creating templates, and as a place to dry fondant and gum-paste decorations. Sifting flour and cocoa directly onto a sheet of parchment makes cleanup go much faster.

2.   LONG METAL RULER: An 18-inch ruler is essential for measuring all aspects of cake and rolled fondant, from guiding the cutting of the cake to measuring the overall height of your cake layers. Metal is preferable because it is much more durable — plastic and wood rulers tend to become cut and dented, which will not give you a perfectly straight edge.

3.   SERRATED KNIFE: This is essential for cutting cakes. It does not compress the cake as a smooth-bladed knife will, and makes carving and sculpting much easier.

4.   SMALL OFFSET SPATULA: This tool is similar to a palette knife, but thicker, and can handle large and heavier cakes and sugar decorations. It is also perfect for mixing colors of Royal Icing, transferring cookies and cakes, frosting cupcakes, spreading icings and preserves, and crumb coating cakes.

5.   LONG OFFSET SPATULA: Approximately 10 inches long, this tool performs the same tasks as the smaller version but can cover more surface area when you are moving or frosting layers of cake. The larger size and longer reach make it useful for releasing dough or cake that is stuck to a surface.

6.   PARING KNIFE: This small, smooth blade is easy to handle and maneuver and is perfect for cutting fondant or gum paste, trimming fondant-covered cakes, and making perfect straight edges.

7.   SCALE: There are several reasons why I prefer to measure my dry ingredients on a scale instead of using measuring cups. A scale gives you accurate measurements, which ensures that your recipes will come out right every time. With measuring cups you can lose count, and depending on how you spoon in the ingredients, the measurements can vary. If you are worried about a scale taking up too much counter space, compact electric scales are available.

8.   FONDANT SMOOTHERS: I am not sure how I ever covered cakes with rolled fondant before I had a pair of these smoothers. These two paddles help smooth bumps and ripples out of the fondant after you place it on the cake. They make a straight, smooth surface, which your hands cannot do. You can also use them to center finished cakes on cake bases or on tiers of cake.

9.   CARDBOARD CAKE BOARDS: Each tier of a cake should have at least one of these boards underneath it (more for cakes larger than 6 inches). This allows you to move your cakes easily and pick them up after they are covered in fondant. In general, you want the cardboard cake board to be the exact size of (or slightly smaller than) your cake layers. With boards underneath, you can glue tiers of cake directly to cake bases, or place a tier directly on top of dowels. You can also make cake boards out of foam core.

10. CUPCAKE WRAPPERS: These paper liners fit into cupcake tins and allow you to handle each individual cupcake. They come in a variety of colors and sizes.

11. WOODEN ROLLING PIN: This traditional wooden rolling pin is tapered at the ends in the French style. It is perfect for rolling out large pieces of cookie dough, rolled fondant, and gum paste.

12. PLASTIC AND WOODEN DOWELS: These dowels provide interior support for your cakes. Use the wider plastic dowels for larger tiers and the skinnier wooden dowels when you do not have as much room to spare. **NEVER** use straws to dowel your cakes. They bend and crack and cause your cakes to collapse.

13. PENCIL SHARPENER: Use this to sharpen the ends of wooden dowels before you insert them into your cakes.

14. RUBBER SPATULA: This tool is handy for scraping batters from bowls, filling pastry bags, and transferring filling from the bowl to the cake.

15. LARGE PIPING TIP: We use these tips often to pipe filling between layers of cake. The large tip helps maintain an even frosting height over the entire cake layer. These tips are also useful for cutting out polka dots and other round sugar decorations.

16. MEASURING SPOONS: These are used to measure small increments of ingredients: 1/8 teaspoon, 1/4 teaspoon, 1/2 teaspoon, 1 teaspoon, and 1 tablespoon. Make sure to level off ingredients before adding them to the recipe.

17. MEASURING CUPS: When you use measuring cups, make sure to spoon in the ingredients with a tablespoon and level off the top with a straight edge in order to get the correct amount.

18. BENCH SCRAPER: This tool is great for keeping a clean work surface at all times. Use it to remove cornstarch and other ingredients from your work table. Its hard metal edge works for cutting fondant and gum paste into individual pieces. I also use this to push Royal Icing from the back of a pastry bag to the front near the tip and get rid of air bubbles.

Decorating Tools

The tools pictured on the following pages are many of the items
I use most often. I refer to them frequently throughout the book.
Having a good collection of decorating tools helps you
complete projects with greater ease.

1. PLASTIC MAT: The smooth surface of this mat is great for rolling out small amounts of gum paste or fondant. Although you can purchase special bakery place mats, any smooth place mat will work fine. Place a flat wet paper towel underneath to prevent the mat from sliding while you are rolling out the dough.

2. PALETTE KNIFE: Use this tool for picking up thinly rolled gum paste or fondant decorations or to get under a cake base or cookie while it is still drying.

3. TAPE MEASURE: A flexible version of a ruler, this tool is invaluable for measuring the curved surfaces of sculpted cakes.

4. PASTRY TIPS: These small metal tips are essential for creating piped designs. You will need a range of sizes, depending on the look you are trying to achieve. Tip sizes are given in numbers; in this book when I say, for example, use a #806 tip or #10 tip, this is what I'm referring to. Always wash and dry pastry tips carefully so they do not rust.

5. PLASTIC COUPLER AND RING: These are used to hold the metal pastry tips on a pastry bag. They also allow you to change a tip without changing the entire bag.

6. LEAF-VEINER MOLD: This silicone mold creates an embossed design on sugar decorations. This particular mold creates the impression of the veins on a leaf. Silicone molds often have two pieces and come in all different forms. They are found in craft and cake-decorating stores.

7. LEAF CUTTER: Use this metal cutter to form the leaves of a plant or flower decoration. The metal cutter gives you the general shape, which you can then press into a silicone mold or shape with your hand.

8. SMALL METAL RULER: A 12-inch ruler is useful for cutting and measuring gum-paste designs. Try to find rulers with no backing. Metal is preferable because plastic and wood rulers tend to get cut and dented, which will not give you a perfectly straight edge.

9. X-ACTO KNIFE: This thin, sharp blade is perfect for creating templates for cookies, cutting intricate sugar decorations, and shaping cardboard and foam core to the exact size you need.

10. SCALPEL: These little knives have become invaluable to me. I first started using them after my dad, who is a surgeon, gave me a few to experiment with. Scalpels have the finest, sharpest blades you can find, so be extremely careful when working with them. They are disposable, so after a few uses you can throw them away. Look for them in medical supply stores.

11. FOOD MARKER: This nontoxic marker allows you to write directly on cakes and decorations just as you would with a real marker. They are great for writing text and drawing fine details, and they are much easier to control than paintbrushes. The ink is completely edible and the markers come in an assortment of colors.

12. TOOTHPICKS: I use toothpicks for transferring food coloring into Royal Icing, fondant, and gum paste. They are also great to use for creating stitching details and veining on leaves, and embossing holes into designs.

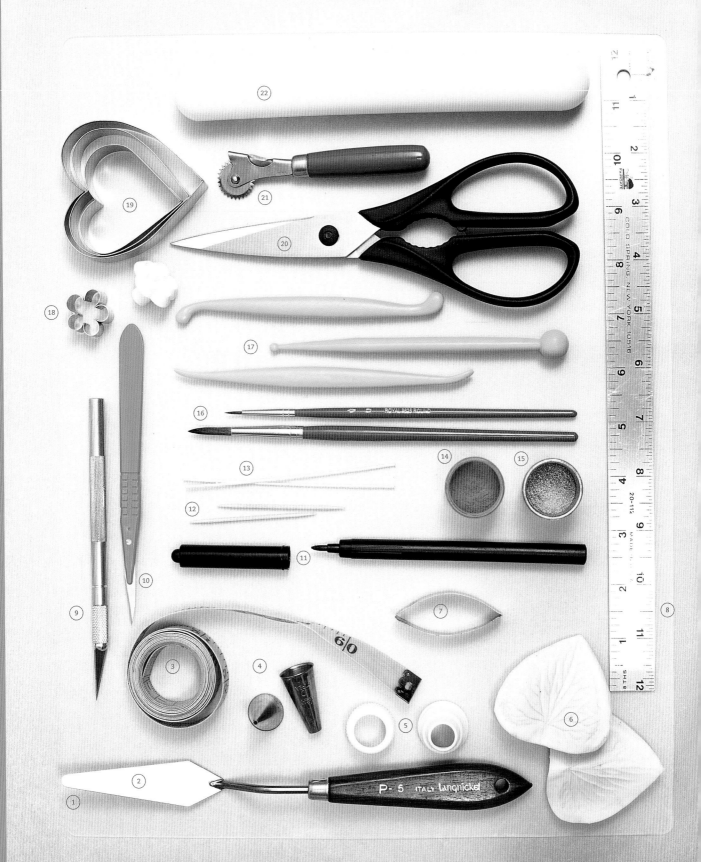

13. CLOTH-COVERED WIRE: This flexible metal wire can be safely inserted directly into your cakes. It comes in both green and white, so consider the colors of your cake and decorations when choosing your wire. It comes in different weights, from #18 gauge (the heaviest) to #28 gauge (the lightest). The heavier your decorations, the stronger the gauge wire you will want to use.

14. PETAL DUST: A nontoxic powder (also known as powdered food coloring) used to decorate dried sugar decorations, petal dust creates a matte finish and is available in many colors. You can apply it with a dry brush or mix it with lemon extract to form a liquid pigment.

15. LUSTER DUST: This nontoxic powder comes in many colors and gives a shiny or metallic look to decorations — use this if you are looking for sparkle on your cake. Luster dust is usually mixed with lemon extract and painted directly on cakes or sugar decorations, but it can also be applied dry.

16. PAINTBRUSHES: Good paintbrushes are instrumental for painting and dusting your cookies, cupcakes, and cakes. Small brushes are best for creating lettering and fine details; larger brushes are great for dry dusting sugar decorations. Make sure that the bristles on the brush come together to form a point if you're creating small details.

17. GUM-PASTE TOOLS: The ball tool, dog-bone tool, and veining tool are used for embossing and sculpting fondant and gum-paste decorations. They are also used for thinning out flower petals and leaves and creating a hollow center in sugar decorations.

18. 5-PETAL CUTTERS: These flower cutters come in both metal and plastic and are useful for creating small sugar decorations. They come in many different shapes and sizes and are often sold in sets.

19. COOKIE CUTTERS: Used for cutting out cookie dough, rolled fondant, and gum paste, these work well whether they are made of metal or plastic.

20. SCISSORS: Sharp scissors are essential for cutting out templates and patterns and for trimming the edges of cake boards.

21. STITCHING TOOL: This wheel, also known as a quilting tool, gives the effect of actual stitching. Use it to give your fondant and sugar decorations details that make them look like fabric or leather.

22. PLASTIC ROLLING PIN: This small white rolling pin is completely smooth and is great for rolling out a small amount of fondant or gum paste on a plastic mat.

Glossary

These general terms are helpful to know before you get started with cake decorating.

Equipment

CAKE BASES: A cake base offers support and an environment for your cake. It allows you to move your project without touching it, and it gives you another surface to decorate. For smaller cakes, create a base out of cardboard or foam core, or use a tray or serving plate. When creating tiered cakes, I suggest using a heavier base made out of wood. This provides a good foundation for the weight of a large cake. You can cover a base in rolled fondant, fabric, paper, or Royal Icing.

CAKE PANS: The best pans are those that do not feel flexible when you pick them up. Heavyweight metal pans tend to produce the most evenly baked product. You can use nonstick pans, but they should still be lined with parchment paper.

DRY PASTRY BRUSH: A wide flat brush, ranging in width from 2 inches to 5 inches, is reserved for brushing away cornstarch when rolling out fondant. You should never wash this brush or get it wet.

ELECTRIC MIXER: A heavy-duty standing mixer is the best for making cakes. It ensures consistency when mixing your ingredients. A handheld mixer will work, but it may be more difficult to control with heavier cookie dough and icing.

FOAM CORE: This all-purpose white craft board with a waxy surface on both sides and a layer of foam in the middle is commonly used to mount artwork and posters, but is also great to use for cake bases and cake boards. Approximately ¼ inch thick, foam core is much stronger than cardboard and provides a good surface for cake layers, and the waxy surface repels moisture and grease better than ordinary cardboard. You can cut it easily with an X-acto knife.

SIEVE: A large, flat-bottomed, round sieve makes sifting all your dry ingredients at once easier. You can hold it with two hands, one on each side. If you do not have a sieve, a sifter can also be used.

SIFTER: Use a sifter to dust your work surface with cornstarch before rolling out fondant.

TURNTABLE: Turntables are great for icing and decorating cakes. They allow you to turn your project from front to back without ever touching it. They also place the cake closer to eye level, which is better for your back and your eyes. Make sure to use a sturdy metal turntable, since plastic ones are flimsy and have a tendency to break or flip over if you are working on a larger cake. If you do not have a turntable, turn over a heavy round cake pan and use that instead.

WET PASTRY BRUSH: This smaller flat brush, 1 inch to 3 inches wide, is great for coating cake pans with butter and for brushing simple syrup onto cake layers. Wash the brush after each use.

WOODEN MALLET OR HAMMER: Use one of these to "hammer" the wooden dowels through your cake layers.

WOODEN SKEWERS: These are used to determine the height of a cake before cutting dowels. Simply stick them into the middle of the cake, mark the top of the cake on the skewer, and pull it out. They can also lend extra support to sugar decorations if you insert them into the middle of the decorations.

Decorating Tools

DRAGÉES: Although dragées are edible, these little ball-shaped decorations do not have a particularly nice flavor or texture, so I use them sparingly. Nothing else gives the same fun metallic look. They come in an assortment of colors, shapes, and sizes.

EGG CARTONS: Recycle your egg cartons — just make sure they are clean! The little egg compartments are perfect for storing dry fondant and gum-paste decorations.

FOOD-COLORING GELS: These highly concentrated food colorings, in liquid or paste, are used to dye fondant, gum paste, Royal Icing, and sanding sugar. You only need a small amount to achieve intense colors. Mix your gels with a small amount of vodka to create a paint.

GLYCERIN: This clear, syruplike substance can be added to fondant that has dried out and started cracking. A small amount of glycerin makes the dough soft and pliable again. You can also use it to make fondant shiny. Just brush it on your cake. Look for glycerin at cake-decorating stores.

LEMON EXTRACT: Pure lemon extract, which has a high concentration of alcohol and therefore evaporates quickly, is the perfect mixing agent to use when painting with food dusts.

PASTRY BAGS: Use these bags to hold the icing or filling when you are piping delicate designs or Royal Icing onto a cookie or creating the perfect swirl of frosting for your cupcakes. They come in lightweight polyurethane or plastic. I prefer the disposable plastic bags — they make cleanup easier and ensure that no fat from the butter in your frosting will touch your Royal Icing. Avoid cloth bags, which are hard on your hands and difficult to clean.

SANDING SUGAR: Used primarily to decorate cookies and the tops of cupcakes, sanding sugar creates a sparkling texture. This fine sugar can be found in a wide array of colors.

SHORTENING: Shortening can be used to coat your plastic mat before rolling fondant and gum paste, to prevent sticking, and is also good for keeping sugar from sticking to molds and fondant or gum paste from sticking to your hands when rolling it into balls and ropes. Shortening is also great for softening hardened gum paste — just knead a little into the hardened ball.

STYROFOAM: This may seem like a strange material to discuss in a pastry book, but cake designers use Styrofoam all the time. Use it to form molds for sugar decorations, such as the Stiletto (page 212). It is easy to carve with a serrated knife, and you can find it in arts-and-crafts stores.

Baking Terms

These are some of the basic elements of our delicious cakes,
and I refer to them frequently throughout the book.

BUTTERCREAM: Because of its body and versatility, this classic frosting is perfect for filling, crumb coating, frosting, and decorating cakes. It can be flavored almost any way you wish (page 56).

CRUMB COAT: Once you have achieved the final shape of your cake, before you apply the outer layer of rolled fondant or icing, you will want to ice your cake with a thin layer of frosting. This smoothes the surface of the cake and seals in the cake crumbs. It also acts like a "glue" to hold the fondant onto the cake (page 34).

ROLLED FONDANT: In this book we use rolled fondant to decorate most of the cookies, cupcakes, and cakes. It is a sweet, pliable dough. The fondant creates a smooth surface that is perfect for adding details. It can also be used to create sugar sculptures and decorations (page 44).

GANACHE: Chocolate ganache is a simple yet rich, delicious, and smooth icing. It can be used as a filling and a frosting. It is made primarily with chopped chocolate and heavy cream—there is no butter involved. It is a nice filling for sculpted cakes because once it cools it's incredibly sturdy (page 57).

GUM PASTE: Gum paste is similar to fondant in terms of texture, but it dries as hard as porcelain. It has incredible elasticity and strength and can be rolled extremely thin without breaking, and sculpted into amazingly detailed shapes. Although gum paste is edible, it is fairly bland, and many of my clients choose to save the gum paste decorations instead of eating them. Store them in an airtight container, away from humidity and moisture.

ROYAL ICING: This thick white icing is used for decorating and constructing cakes. This icing starts off soft but dries hard, and is the edible "glue" that adheres cake tiers and is used to pipe designs and ice cookies. Royal Icing can be dyed any color with food-coloring gels and piped into any shape imaginable. It is just about the sweetest thing around because its primary ingredient is confectioners' sugar (page 58).

SIMPLE SYRUP: All of our cake recipes are moist on their own, but if you feel like adding a hint of flavor without incorporating it into the entire recipe, you can apply a layer of flavored simple syrup. You make it by boiling equal amounts of water and sugar together (page 59). Once it is cool, add the extract or liquor of your choice to flavor it. Use a pastry brush to spread the syrup over layers of cake before adding your filling.

Practical Matters

One of the most important parts of successful cake decorating
is making a plan well in advance and sticking to it.
Here is what you need to include in your plan, and how to
deal with other practicalities of cake design.

Make a Plan

Decorated cakes have so many different elements that it is easy to feel over-whelmed. Before you even buy the ingredients for your cake the most important thing to do is make a plan. Either find a photograph or sketch the design of the cake you have decided to make. Look at the picture and think about what needs to be done first. For example, if there are many sugar decorations, you should start with these since they will need time to dry. These are the things your plan should take into account.

SERVINGS: First you need to determine how many people the cake needs to serve. The size of your cake is going to affect everything from the base you place it on to the number of sugar decorations you need to the size of the box you will need to carry it out the door. The servings for single and multitiered cakes are easier to figure out than sculpted cakes. For each project in this book, we tell you how many servings it provides. But if you are doing something on your own, all you need to do when making a tiered cake is add the servings together of each tier (refer to page 59 for the serving size chart). For sculpted cakes

you want to bake more cake than you need to allow for extra room to carve away. You might make the cutest-looking cake ever, but if there is not enough for everyone to eat you will be sorry!

BASES: Next you need to determine what your cake will sit on. The base is a crucial element for decorating and transporting the finished cake. Do not spend hours working on a cake that you cannot move! For heavier cakes we suggest using a wood base (you can cover it to make it look pretty). For smaller cakes you can use foiled cardboard bases found at decorating stores or make your own using layers of cardboard glued together and covered in fondant, fabric, decorative paper, or foil. At Confetti Cakes, we cover all the bases for our cakes in fondant. This gives the cleanest look and incorporates the base into the cake's overall color and decoration scheme. We suggest covering the base at least one day ahead of time so the cake will not disturb the base's fondant when it is placed on top.

SUGAR DECORATIONS: Decorations created out of gum paste or fondant usually need a few days to dry before you can apply them to your cake. Once you determine how many decorations you need, make them ahead of time and set them aside to dry.

BAKING THE CAKES: Always keep your final design plan in mind. Take into consideration the final shape of the cake and try to match your pan as closely to the final shape as possible. For example, if you use a round pan for a square design, you will be left with tons of excess cake. The best pan to use for an irregular design or a design that is pieced together is a half sheet.

MAKING THE FILLINGS: While your cakes are cooling, whip up your filling and frosting. You may decide to use just one flavor to fill and crumb coat your cake or you can layer different flavors on separate layers or tiers.

Transporting Cookies, Cupcakes, and Cakes

After spending hours working on your beautiful creations the last thing you want to happen is for anything to get damaged during transport. Bakery boxes are good for smaller items, but I prefer heavy, two-layer corrugated boxes, which are more sturdy than typical cake boxes. No matter what you are carrying them in, make sure the box stays level! Here are a few more tips for specific types of confections.

COOKIES: Make sure they are completely dry before bagging or boxing, separating each layer with a piece of parchment paper.

CUPCAKES: Refrigerate cupcakes before boxing them. When you place them in the box, make sure the bottom is completely flat and sturdy. Create one row of cupcakes then make a second row by placing cupcakes between two cupcakes in the first row. This will help keep them from shifting in the box.

CAKES: Use an ordinary corrugated box, two inches wider than your cake base. If you are creating a cake that is more than four tiers high, or if you have fragile or heavy sugar decorations, assemble the cake once you arrive at your location.

1. Put the box together, making sure to reinforce the bottom with packing tape.

2. Cut open one side of the box, so you can slide the cake in and keep it level.

3. Before placing the cake inside the box, put some packing tape in the middle of the box, sticky side up. When the cake is centered in the box the cake base will stick to the tape and prevent the cake from sliding. Tape the box closed.

4. Place the cake in your car with protection on all sides to keep the box from shifting.

5. When you arrive at your location, find out where the cake will be going before taking it out of the car. When you've reached your final destination, carefully cut all the sides of the box open and use an offset spatula to lift the cake out of the box, removing the tape from the bottom of the base.

If Disaster Strikes

WARNING: You might spend days in the kitchen creating your masterpiece, but if a huge accident — such as a collapse — occurs, there is probably little you can do to repair your cake, and it might be best to start over. That said, if something less than disastrous happens, such as a shift in tiers during transportation, a crack in the fondant, or a sugar decoration breaking off, do not let your emotions get the best of you. Take a deep breath and make a game plan. You may be surprised how much of the cake can be salvaged. It could be as simple as adding some decorations to cover a crack. Pay attention to what caused the problem so you can avoid it in the future!

When to Use Fondant vs. Gum Paste

Fondant is a sweet, soft dough that is quite malleable and stays relatively soft after it has set; it is best used to cover an entire cake. Gum paste, also referred to as sugar dough, contains an edible chemical called gum tragacanth that allows the dough to be rolled out very thin but makes it dry very hard. Gum paste should be used for highly detailed decorations or decorations that need to stand on their own structurally, such as a flower, bag handle, or shoe. For the most part, these two doughs are not interchangeable, as a detailed decoration in fondant will not hold its shape, and a cake covered in gum paste, aside from not tasting very good, would be as hard as porcelain and nearly impossible to cut.

Storing Fondant and Gum Paste

Both fondant and gum paste dry out quickly. The worst thing is to find your fondant or gum paste has dried out, especially when you have already mixed the perfect color. Even if you are just taking a short break or working on another part of the cake, keep them tightly wrapped in plastic wrap. When you are finished using them for the day, double wrap them in plastic wrap and place them in an airtight container. Never get fondant or gum paste wet, because they become too sticky to handle. Store gum paste and fondant at room temperature.

Once you have finished decorating your cake in rolled fondant or gum paste, do not store it in the refrigerator. The extra humidity makes the cake sweat and could cause your gum-paste decorations to wither. Store the cake, uncovered, in an air-conditioned room or the coolest spot in your house.

HOT TIPS

■ If the gum paste you have rolled out is drying too quickly, cover the mat with a piece of plastic wrap and place a damp cloth on top of the plastic, never letting the water touch the gum paste.

■ If you are making a lot of gum-paste decorations and you want them to dry as quickly as possible, use a dehumidifier!

Techniques

These are the key techniques you will need to use
for many projects throughout the book.

Cookie Techniques

Flooding

Flooding is a method of frosting cookies
that enables you to **create a smooth,
well-defined, glossy icing finish.**

What You Need

Undecorated cookies

2 pastry bags

#2 pastry tip

#3 pastry tip

Stiff Royal Icing

Loose Royal Icing

Toothpicks

1. Fill a pastry bag fitted with a #2
pastry tip with stiff Royal Icing. Using
the shape of the cookie as your guide,
pipe a complete outline of the cookie.
Make sure there are no gaps in the
outline, or your "flood" will spill outside
the line. Wait a few minutes before
flooding the cookie to let the outline set.

2. Using the second pastry bag fitted
with a #3 tip filled with the loose icing,
pipe icing in the center of the cookie.
Bring the icing right up to the piped
outline by using a toothpick to help
drag the icing to the edge. Do this
fairly quickly so the icing doesn't
set before you've covered the entire
surface. The flooded area should be
about ⅛ inch thick.

3. Let the cookies dry for about 20
minutes before serving. If you are
adding decorations, let them dry for
about 3 hours. If you are planning to
package your cookies to transport, send,
or present them, let them dry overnight.

HOT TIPS

■ Loose Royal Icing should have an
almost runny consistency. Add water,
just a little at a time, to stiff Royal
Icing to achieve this effect. To test
for the correct consistency, draw
a knife through the icing; the knife
mark should disappear after about
5 seconds. If it doesn't, add water,
one drop at a time, until you get to
the right consistency.

■ If you are using the flooding method
to decorate a large number of cookies,
create all the outlines first, then do all
the flooding.

Drop-in Flooding

Use this method to **drop one or more additional colors into your flooded background.** You will need to do the drop-in flooding quickly, so be prepared with the second color of flood (or looser icing) already in a pastry bag.

Once you have flooded the cookie with one color, squeeze a small amount of the second color icing right into the initial layer of icing **while it is still wet.** Create polka dots or swirl patterns for a smooth patterned look. See the Dragonfly and Butterfly cookies (page 91) for examples.

HOT TIP

■ If you want to use the drop-in flooding method, try to stay away from dark colors, because they tend to bleed.

Overpiping

Use this technique to create a **raised border or three-dimensional design** on flooded cookies.

What You Need

Flooded cookies

Pastry bag, filled with stiff Royal Icing fitted with #2 tip (or larger tip if a thicker line is desired)

Method

1. Make sure the flooded cookie has dried for at least 10 minutes.

2. Use the same color you used to flood or a contrasting color of icing to pipe directly on top of the original outline to create a raised border, or use it to add design details, monograms, or piped bows on top of the flood.

Decorating with Sanding Sugar

This process, which **leaves cookies with a sparkly layer,** reminds me of being in art class when I was younger. I would spread glue onto a piece of paper and coat it with glitter. Once the glue dried, I would pour the excess glitter away and be left with a shimmering work of art.

What You Need

Flooded cookies OR cookies brushed with hot preserves

Sanding sugar

Small bowl

Spoon

Method

While the Royal Icing (or heated preserves) on the cookie are **still wet,** spoon on a thick layer of sanding sugar and wait at least 20 minutes for the icing or preserves to dry. Tip the cookie to remove the excess sugar.

HOT TIPS

▪ You can save the excess sugar to use again if it is not attached to any Royal Icing. Just be sure to let the icing or preserves dry completely.

▪ If you have only white sanding sugar you can make your own variety of colors by using vodka and food coloring. Check out the method for dyeing the rock candy crystals that we use with our Crystal Cupcakes (page 96) to learn how.

Making a Template

Using a metal cookie cutter makes preparing a large number of cookies easy. If you are making only a small number of cookies and you want to **design your own shapes,** you can make a cookie template.

What You Need

A shape or design

A piece of foam core or cardboard

X-acto knife

Scissors

Rolled-out cookie dough

Method

Trace or draw your design right onto a piece of foam core or cardboard and cut out the shape with an X-acto knife. Trim with scissors if you need to. Place the template on top of your rolled-out cookie dough and use the X-acto knife to cut the shape out of the dough. Transfer to a cookie sheet with an offset spatula and bake as you would any cookie-cutter cookies.

HOT TIP

▪ Dip your template in flour before using it, to prevent your dough from sticking to the cutout.

Cupcake Techniques

Creating a Dome of Filling

When a recipe requires **covering your cupcakes** in fondant, brown sugar, or chocolate "dirt," you want a nice smooth surface to start with. A dome of filling, whether buttercream, ganache, or frosting, is the perfect solution.

What You Need

Baked cupcakes

Filling of choice

Small offset spatula

Method

Pipe or spoon a small amount of frosting onto a cupcake. Starting in the middle of the cupcake, use a small offset spatula to pull the icing out evenly toward all edges of the cupcake and create a smooth, domed surface ½ inch thick.

HOT TIP

■ Cupcakes always look a little better if the tops come to just below the edge of the wrapper before you frost. To achieve this, fill the wrappers only halfway with batter before baking. You may want to do a test of how high to fill the batter with one cupcake before baking all of them.

Creating a Swirl of Frosting

A swirl is a beautiful way to decorate a cupcake. It doesn't need any other adornment! This is a tricky piping technique so practice it before you attempt it on an actual cupcake. If you make a mistake, just give the cupcake a shake over the bowl to remove the buttercream and reuse, as long as there are no cake crumbs in it.

What You Need

Baked cupcakes

Buttercream

Pastry bag

#806 pastry tip (or other large pastry tip)

Method

1. Spoon the buttercream into a pastry bag fitted with a #806 tip.

2. Start at the outer edge of the cupcake and slowly move the bag in a clockwise motion, piping the icing onto the cupcake.

3. Each time you pass your starting point, the swirl should be getting smaller and going higher. Usually it takes about 3 revolutions until you get to the top of the swirl.

Covering Cupcakes in Fondant

Fondant is not just for cakes! You can create miniature works of art by covering cupcakes in fondant.

What You Need

Baked cupcakes with smooth domes of filling

Fondant

2½-inch round cutter (for standard cupcakes)

Paring knife

Method

On a surface coated with shortening or cornstarch, roll out the fondant to approximately ⅛ inch thick. Use the cutter to cut out rounds of fondant. Place the rounds of fondant on top of the frosted cupcakes. Gently smooth the fondant toward the edges. Cut away any excess fondant with a paring knife.

Cake and Mini Cake Techniques

Splitting Cake

What You Need

Baked cake

Serrated knife

Cake board

Method

1.   If a cake has risen unevenly, use a long serrated knife to cut off the top domed surface. This gives you a flat top surface to work with.

2.   Using the serrated knife, cut through the cake horizontally to create two 1-inch-thick layers.

3.   Transfer the layer that you plan to use on the bottom to a cake board, attaching the layer to the board with a dab of buttercream.

HOT TIP

■ For big cakes, ahead of time glue together at least three cardboard layers (in the shape and size of the bottom cake layer) before placing the cake on top. This gives extra stability.

Filling Cake

What You Need

Split cake

Filling of your choice

Offset spatula

Method

1. Aim for layers of filling that are half as thick as your layers of cake (for 1-inch cake layers, make ½-inch layers of filling). This ensures a tasty ratio of cake to filling in every bite.

2. Spread the filling to within ½ inch of the cake edge. This will ensure that the filling will not spill out from the sides when the next layer is placed on top.

3. Alternate cake layers with filling layers until you place your last layer of cake on top.

HOT TIP

When I'm making a multitiered cake, I often use three layers of cake with two layers of frosting in one tier.

Sculpting Cake

You can create just about any shape you want out of cake. To make a sculpted cake, first assess the general shape of what you will be carving. This will allow you to determine what cake to use.

• For a ball or an oval-like shape, bake the cakes in round pans.

• For any other shape I suggest using half sheet pans (13 x 18 inches). Although pans come in different shapes, due to shrinkage and uneven baking I find them difficult to use. Half sheets allow the cake to bake evenly and you can cut any size imaginable from the rectangle shape.

• Once you have cut out the general shape of the cakes, layer them with frosting just like a regular round cake. When carving the cake into a specific shape you want to start with larger pieces than you may think necessary. Sculpting cakes is similar to carving an ice sculpture — start with a large block of cake and carve away a little at a time with a serrated knife.

• After the cake shape is completely sculpted you may need to trim your cake board with a serrated knife to meet the edge of the cake.

• Crumb coat the cake and cover it with fondant. Depending on the shape of the cake, you may decide to cover the entire cake with one piece of fondant or you may want to cover it in separate pieces.

Doweling Sculpted Cakes

If you are creating a sculpted cake taller than 4 inches you need to dowel the cake for support before adding your extra layers. (See page 37.) Before covering the cake with fondant, insert dowels directly into the bottom layer and then place a piece of foam core that has been cut into the shape of the cake beneath the next layers. Make sure to cut the foam core an inch smaller than your cake on each side so it does not interfere with your carving.

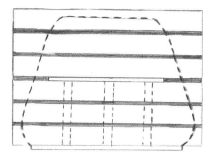

Crumb Coating

This technique smoothes the outside of your cake and gets it ready to be covered in fondant.

What You Need

Split and filled (and sculpted, if you are sculpting) cake

Small serrated knife

Offset spatula

Method

1. If necessary, use a small serrated knife to trim any protruding edges that are not part of your intended shape. To create a perfectly smooth fondant-covered cake, you need a uniform crumb coat.

2. Using an offset spatula, smooth any of the extra filling coming out from the inside layers, plus a little more filling, into a thin layer over the outside of your cake. Create an even surface all over the cake. If you have time, let the cake sit overnight so that it can settle before you cover it with fondant.

Covering Cake with Fondant

When you have **crumb coated the cake and the cake board is trimmed you are ready to cover your cake with fondant.** I think of this as the second phase of your cake design. Your work space should be completely clean and free of cake, crumbs, and filling.

This is the basic method for covering a round cake. Most people find round cakes to be the easiest to cover because the fondant drapes over the edges easily. The methods for cakes in other shapes are not much different — follow these steps and see the sections on square cakes, irregularly shaped cakes, and piecing fondant (page 36), as appropriate.

What You Need

Split, filled, shaped, and crumb coated cake

Strainer

Cornstarch

Fondant in the amount and colors your project requires

Rolling pin

Dry pastry brush

Fondant smoothers

Paring knife

Method

1. Using a small strainer, dust a clean, flat surface with cornstarch. This prevents the fondant from sticking to the work surface.

2. Unwrap the fondant from the plastic wrap, and knead it into a malleable dough. Shape it into a flattened round ball.

3. Using a rolling pin, roll out the fondant much in the way you would roll out cookie dough. In the beginning, give the fondant a few turns to ensure it is even on all sides. Roll it out larger than the area you need to cover, and approximately ¼ inch thick. When considering how wide you should roll it, be sure to take into consideration the height of the sides of the cake as well as the top surface.

4. While the fondant is still on the flat surface, run the fondant smoothers over it to even it out.

5. To pick up the fondant, roll it onto a rolling pin, wiping off any extra cornstarch with a dry pastry brush as you go. Once all of the fondant is around the pin, carefully unroll it over the cake.

6. Start at the top and smooth the surface of the fondant with your hands. Continue along the sides of the cake, gently pressing the fondant to the shape of the cake. Be careful not to press the fondant onto itself; it will wrinkle. Gently pull the fondant away from the cake before smoothing it back down, the way you smooth the pleats of a skirt, **after** the cake is completely covered. Use the fondant smoothers to help create a smooth surface by rubbing them all over the cake.

7. When the entire cake is covered, cut away any excess fondant with a paring knife. The cleanest way to do this is first to cut away the majority of fondant but leave approximately a 1-inch border. Using the side of your hand, gently press the remaining excess fondant against the bottom of the cake where it meets the cake board, to form a small crease. Make a final cut around the entire bottom of the cake, leaving a perfectly smooth edge.

HOT TIP

■ If you have the time, let fondant-covered cakes sit overnight. This gives the cake a chance to settle before decorating and makes it easier to handle.

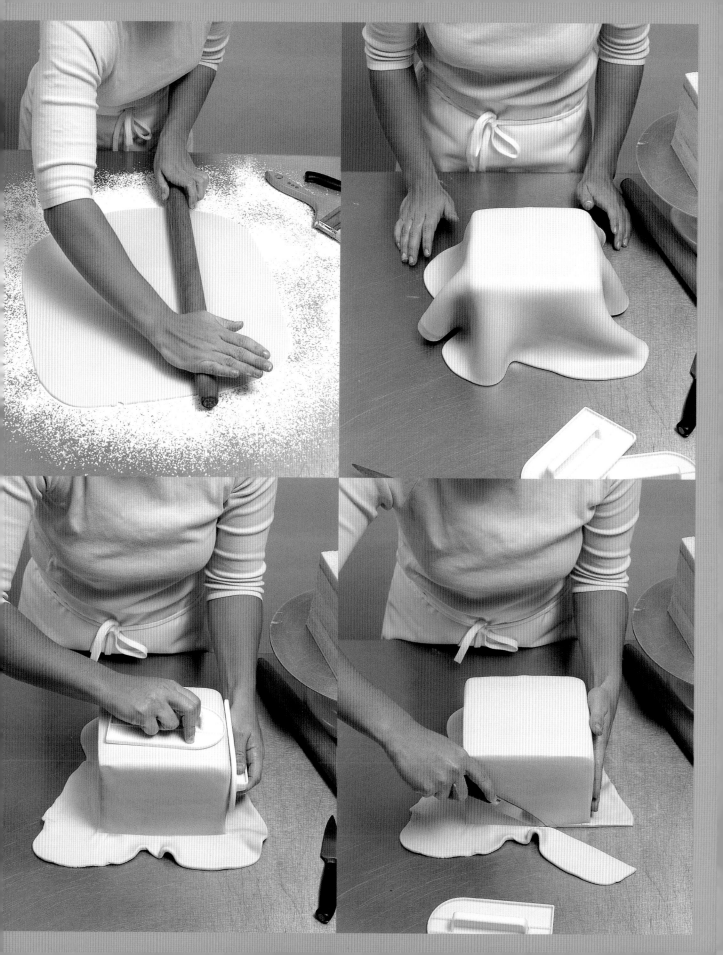

Square Cakes

When covering square cakes, pay close attention to the corners — if the fondant is too heavy or dry, the corners of your cake might be weighed down or the edges might begin to crack. To prevent this, make sure your fondant is rolled to ¼ inch — not thicker — and it is not too dry. (You know it is too dry if it's is cracking before you even roll it out.) If it feels dry to you, knead a little shortening or glycerin into it and try to work quickly.

As soon as you cover the cake, use a combination of your hands and the fondant smoothers to press the fondant into the sides of the cake and manipulate it into the proper shape around the corners.

Sculpted and Irregular Shape Cakes

For cakes in unusual shapes such as a sphere or a bell, your best bet may still be to cover the entire cake at once. If the cake is too tall or too wide for that, consider piecing fondant together.

Piecing Fondant

This is a great technique to use when you want to create the look of a box or a bag, especially when the top will be covered in something other than fondant. If you decide to piece fondant, try to join it in places that would be a natural seam for whatever you are covering. This way it will be less obvious.

1. Roll out the fondant on a cutting board covered in shortening, to prevent sticking.

2. Use a paring knife and a ruler to cut out separate pieces and place the board in the freezer for at least 15 minutes to harden. This makes pieces easier to handle.

3. Slide an offset spatula under the pieces to release the fondant from the board and gently apply it to your cake. If the fondant is not sticking, add more filling. That means the cake has been sitting too long.

Covering Cake Base with Fondant

To create a cake base, brush your cake board with water and cover it with fondant rolled to ⅛ inch thick, smoothing and cutting the edges just as if it were a real cake. Set it aside to dry for at least a few hours and preferably overnight before stacking cakes on top.

Making a Structurally Sound Cake

Sometimes I think I should have been an architect. The most important element of your cake (aside from delicious flavor) is structural security. To keep your creation safe, there are many factors to consider. The weather could make the fillings melt. Your dog could decide to take a bite. There's not much you can do about your dog. But there are a few things you can do to create a stable environment for your cake. From cutting your cake straight to making your filling properly, you need to take each component seriously and do it right.

Always store your cake at the proper temperature. Cold is always better than hot, and fondant-covered cakes like to be stored in a cool or air-conditioned room. I do not suggest a refrigerator because of the humidity. Once you remove it from the fridge, a fondant-covered cake will begin to sweat, and that might ruin your sugar decorations. The density of cakes is important, too. Your cake shouldn't be dry and heavy — but a very delicate or superlight or crumbly cake just won't work for sculpting. And the main issue that leads to cake disasters is weak internal structure. To keep the cake structure strong, we dowel cakes that are over 4 inches high.

Doweling Tiered Cakes

Creating a cake of more than one tier does not require defying gravity, just careful planning. There is an old theory that you can use heavy plastic drinking straws to dowel your cakes. I would **not** advise this. The straws can crack easily, and when they are inserted into a very moist cake, they have the habit of sliding, which creates a horrible threat to the architecture of your cake.

The best dowels are plastic tubes, which are very strong and can handle even the heaviest of cakes. You can find them either in cake-decorating stores (see Resources) or hardware stores. If you cannot find plastic dowels the second-best choice is wooden dowels, which you can find at any hardware store. No matter which kind you use, you will need to cut them to the exact height of the tiers into which you'll be inserting them.

HOT TIP

■ We often use a combination of plastic and wooden dowels. We choose wooden dowels when we are creating a smaller cake because they are thinner. The plastic ones are much wider and take up more room.

■ To dowel your cakes, make sure each tier (or every 4 inches of cake) has a few cake boards underneath for support.

Method

1. Glue the bottom tier of cake (remember, each tier of cake is on its own board) onto your cake base. You can achieve this with nontoxic white glue. (Do not worry — no one will be eating the cardboard under your cake!)

2. Insert a wooden skewer or cloth-covered wire into the center of the cake. Using a pencil or pen make a mark where the top of your cake hits the skewer. Pull out the skewer and use this as a guide to cut the dowels to size with a serrated knife or small handsaw. The number of dowels you cut depends on the size of your cake and the size of the next tier.

3. Place one dowel in the center and a ring of five or six dowels around. If the tier gets much wider, create another ring, being careful not to go outside the size of the next tier. For example, if you are placing a 9-inch tier on top of a 12-inch tier, you do not want your dowels placed outside the 9-inch round or you will be able to see them. To avoid confusion, use a cardboard round or the bottom of the cake pan of the next size tier to create an imaginary border.

4. Once you have the dowels inserted straight into the cake, spread Royal Icing all over the doweled area, again being careful not to go outside the line of the next tier.

5. Using a palette knife, carefully lay the next tier on top and center it (see illustration page 183). Use your hands or fondant smoothers to adjust the cake. The Royal Icing does not dry instantly so you have a few minutes to adjust the tier.

6. If you are creating a cake more than two tiers high, repeat steps 2, 3, and 4. Do not dowel the top tier of a cake unless you plan to place a heavy ornament or sugar sculpture on top.

7. If you are creating a cake more than two tiers high, I suggest placing one long dowel through the entire height of the cake. This is especially important if you are transporting the cake, as it will prevent the cake from shifting during transportation. To do this, measure the height of the cake, not including the base. Cut the dowel to the proper length and use a pencil sharpener to sharpen one end of the dowel. Guide the sharpened point straight into the center of the top tier until you feel it hit the first cardboard. Using a wooden mallet or hammer, guide the dowel straight down through the entire cake.

Deconstructing Cakes

Because so many of these cakes look like real objects, it is not always obvious how to cut them. When you are at a party serving your fabulous cake, you need to know how to dismantle it so people can taste how delicious it is.

If your cake is made out of distinct tiers, slide a knife under the cardboard of each tier and remove it before cutting. Start at the top and lift each tier as you work your way down. If a cake is made out of two layers within the inside of the cake (like the handbag cake) and it is not clear where the dowels are, cut straight down until you hit cardboard. Serve the slices on that tier, remove the cake cardboard, dowels, and any sugar decorations attached with wire, and continue cutting the next tier.

For cakes that have been created out of multiple pieces of cake and sugar, such as our Sugar Stiletto and Shoebox cake (page 212), it is best to deconstruct the entire cake before serving it.

Decorating Techniques

Filling a Pastry Bag

What You Need

Scissors

10-inch pastry bag

Coupler

Pastry tip(s)

Small rubber spatula

Royal Icing (page 58)

Method

1. Using the scissors, cut off the tip of the disposable icing bag and discard.

2. Separate the ring from the bottom of the coupler and insert the bottom piece of the coupler into the piping bag. The bottom piece should fit into the tip of the bag.

3. Place the decorating tip onto the coupler and screw the ring over the tip. Make sure there is a tight fit so no icing spills out of the bag.

4. Have your rubber spatula and icing next to you and ready to go. Form your hand into a C-shape and place the large, open end of the piping bag around the outside of your hand.

5. Fill the bag with icing, using the rubber spatula. The C-shape of your hand should form a rim to scrape the spatula against as the icing falls into the bag. Do not fill the bag more than halfway with stiff icing; your hand will ache, and you will have less control when piping.

6. Using the spatula or your hand, push all the icing down toward the tip of the bag. Twist the bag closed and hold it closed as you pipe so extra icing does not squirt out the back of the bag. Keep the bag twisted when it is on the counter by folding the back of the bag under the icing.

HOT TIP

▐ While you're not using it, cover the Royal Icing with a damp cloth to keep it from drying out.

Piping

Piping can be one of the most difficult decorating techniques to master. It requires great concentration and hand-eye coordination. The best way to learn is by practicing. Back in pastry school we would practice on pieces of parchment paper and then on the sides of cake pans. I find it helps if I hold my breath while I pipe because it keeps my hands steady. But don't forget to take breaks and breathe!

What You Need

Filled pastry bag

Round decorating tips (#2 or #3)

Method

DOTS

The most important factor when piping dots is the pressure you apply to the back of the pastry bag. You want to start applying pressure at a 45-degree angle until you achieve the size bead you want and then gradually release the pressure **before** you pull the bag away. If you pull the bag away too soon, your dots will form peaks. If you think you are applying the correct pressure and you are still getting peaks, then you may need to create a looser icing by adding water a drop at a time until you achieve the desired consistency.

STRAIGHT LINES

Making straight lines can be tough because it is so easy for your hands to shake. Start with the piping bag at a 45-degree angle and hold your elbows close to your body so there is something to ground you. Touch the cake surface, squeeze with constant pressure, and lift the piping tip away from the surface, letting the icing fall while you move your hands toward where you will end. Always keep your eyes moving from where you start to where you will finish — that way you will not be surprised when you reach the end of the line. Avoid dragging the piping tip. If you are creating an outline on a cookie, it is best to use the outer edge of the cookie as a guide.

SWAGS

Start as you would for a straight line, touching the surface of the cake and pull away from the cake as you move sideways. Let the icing drop until it achieves the desired length. Keep pressure constant at all times. If you are creating a design around a circular cake or cookie you may want to indicate where each swag will begin and end by marking evenly sized intervals. If the swag line breaks or comes out the wrong size just use a toothpick to lift off the unwanted string and begin again.

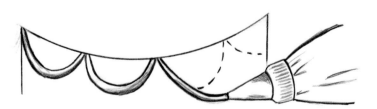

Dyeing Fondant and Gum Paste

Using white fondant or gum paste with food colorings, you can create decorations in **any color you want.**

What You Need

Fondant or gum paste

Toothpick

Gel or liquid food coloring

Method

1. Place your fondant or gum paste on a clean surface. Use a toothpick to add a tiny dab of coloring directly to it. Food coloring is highly concentrated, so you do not need to add much to get a lot of color. Start with a tiny amount and add more if you need it.

2. Knead until the coloring is completely worked through. It is usually best to start with a small piece to achieve the exact shade you desire. If you are trying to achieve a marbleized look, stop kneading as soon as the color is worked in evenly as stripes, and roll it out before the color becomes too uniform.

Dyeing Royal Icing and Buttercream

Start with white Royal Icing or buttercream. **Always divide your icing into separate containers before coloring it,** and save a little extra white icing in case you make a mistake. You can find food-coloring gels in cake-decorating or craft stores, or online (see Resources, page 218).

What You Need

Toothpick

Food-coloring gels

Royal Icing or buttercream

Palette knife or offset spatula

Method

1. Dip the end of a toothpick into the coloring just until the end is lightly coated, about ¼ inch up the toothpick, and dab the color into the icing.

2. Using a palette knife or offset spatula, mix the coloring until it becomes a uniform, solid color. To achieve a darker color, repeat this process, adding the color a little bit at a time (it is always easier to darken than to lighten).

HOT TIPS

▮ It is very difficult to lighten a color by adding white icing to a dark color. You are better off starting with a clean container of white icing.

▮ Add color GRADUALLY until you achieve the color you desire. Be PATIENT when mixing colors. This is an extremely important and time-consuming part of decorating.

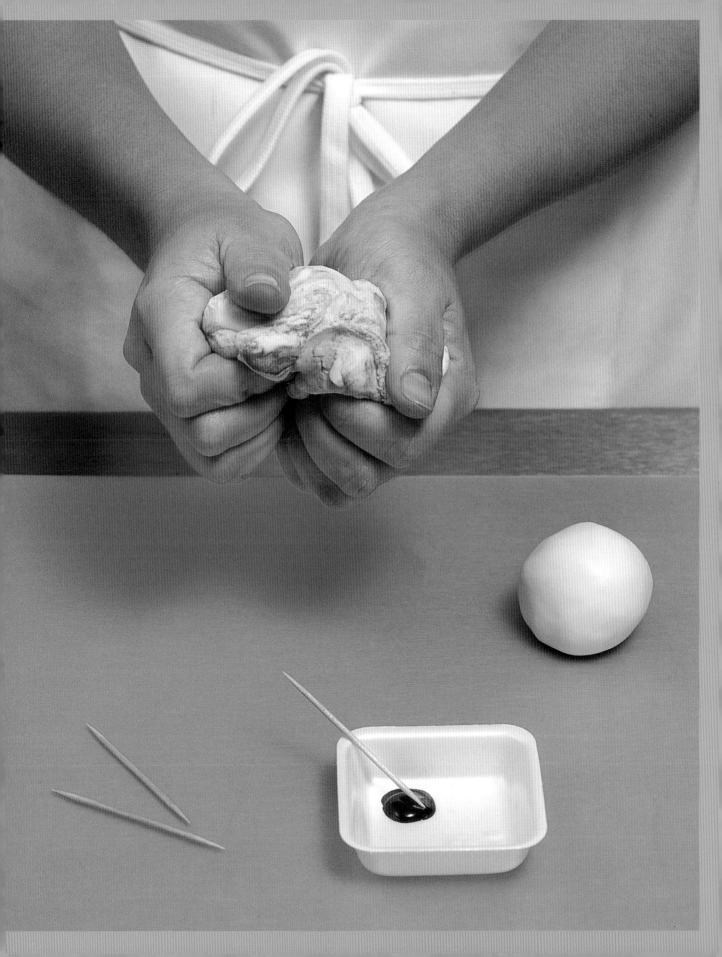

Wood Staining

Our wood-staining technique is inspired by the French art form *trompe l'oeil,* which literally means "to trick the eye." This technique makes rolled fondant look exactly like a wooden surface. We use this for cake bases or to create the look of wooden wine crates, the bark on a tree, and wooden sushi platters. The amount of materials you'll need depends on whether you're staining something small like chopsticks or something big like a cake base.

What You Need

Rolled fondant in white and light brown

Brown food coloring

Rolling pin

Paintbrush with stiff bristles

Vodka

Method

1. Using the white rolled fondant and brown food coloring, mix half of the total fondant light brown.

2. Roll the fondant into 2 long skinny ropes, one from light brown fondant and one from white fondant.

3. Using the white fondant as your base color, twist the fondants together, so the brown becomes marbled into the white. Be careful not to overtwist — leave some of the white fondant showing to create the irregular markings of the wood.

4. Roll out the fondant and place it either on a cake or a board.

5. In a small dish, mix 2 tablespoons vodka and a small drop of brown food coloring. Paint a thin coat over the entire surface.

6. Add more food coloring to the mixture to make a darker brown, and paint smaller irregular markings, just as you would see in real wood.

HOT TIPS

▪ Find an actual piece of wood, even a wooden cutting board, or a photograph. Using the wood as a model while you paint helps you create a defined and realistic pattern.

▪ To make the wood look rustic, take your paring knife and make rough markings all over the surface of the fondant before you paint.

Brush Embroidery

This is a beautiful technique that allows you to create delicate designs involving flowers and other organic elements. The end result can even give you the look of real china. See the Teacups (page 152) and Two-Tiered Cake (page 180) for examples.

What You Need

Royal Icing (see page 58)

#2, #3, or #4 tip

Pastry bag and coupler

Water or pasteurized egg whites

Small paintbrushes

Method

1. Pipe the outline of the design with Royal Icing, one section at a time.

2. Dip the brush in water or egg whites and pull the icing from the middle of the line in one smooth stroke so it is thick from where you start and fades to a thin transparency.

3. In the finished design, leave the brushstrokes to provide texture and give the design a painterly look.

Butterflies

Using this technique you can create a beautiful butterfly.

1. First pipe the head and body.

2. Create the outline for the wings.

3. Pull the icing to create delicate, transparent wings.

HOT TIPS

■ The Royal Icing must be thin enough to be brushed smoothly but not so thin that it can't hold its shape. If the icing is too thin, add either more stiff icing or sifted confectioners' sugar.

■ To transfer a pattern onto the cake, emboss the design you desire onto the cake with a toothpick.

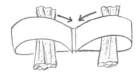

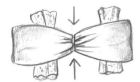

Making Sugar Bows

These gum-paste decorations are perfect for all kinds of cakes and cookies, especially the mini present cakes. You can cut bows and ribbons to fit a cake of any shape or size. This version will fit on a 3 x 3-inch present cake (page 136).

What You Need

Parchment paper

Paper towels

Gum paste

Plastic place mat

Shortening

Small rolling pin

Paring knife

Small dish of water or egg whites

Method

1. Prepare a sheet or flat surface with parchment paper for the pieces to rest before assembly. Roll a few paper towels into logs and set aside.

2. On a greased place mat, roll ¼ pound of gum paste into a sheet approximately ⅛ inch thick. Cut out a 2 x 9-inch strip.

3. Bring the two ends of the strip together at the center, draping the loops of the bows over the paper-towel balls to keep them from collapsing. Attach the ends at the center using a few drops of water or egg white. Pinch the center to create the look of a real ribbon tied into a bow.

4. Cut out another small strip of gum paste approximately ¾ inch wide and long enough to wrap around the center of the ribbon. Wrap it around the center of the bow.

5. To make the ribbon tails, cut a 6 x ¾-inch strip of gum paste and cut the strip in half. Cut out a triangle from the bottom of each tail. Let them dry on top of rolled paper towels, allowing them to lie just as a real ribbon would, making sure that the ends that will sit under the bow are flat.

6. When you are ready to assemble the bow and ribbons, attach the two ribbon tails to the cake with Royal Icing, then lay the bow on top of the two tails, hiding where they are connected so they look like they were tied together out of one piece of ribbon.

Making Party Streamers

This is a fun and easy way to enhance cakes with color. Use them as adornments for any fun cake or group of cupcakes in this book.

What You Need

Gum paste

Paring knife

Paintbrushes

Shortening

Method

1.   Roll out ⅛-inch-thick sheets of gum paste. Using a paring knife, cut all different lengths and widths from your rolled-out sheet.

2.   Coat the backs of paintbrush handles or wooden dowels with shortening and wrap the gum paste around them. You can wrap them tightly together or twist them around the dowel on a diagonal.

3.   After approximately 30 minutes, remove the streamers from the handles or dowels and, if desired, pull them slightly apart or even curve them into any shape you like. (They will feel like an accordion so push and pull as you wish.) Let them dry for another few hours or, if it is humid, a few days.

Basic Recipes

Basic Recipes

Our cakes and cookies are known for being as delicious as they are beautiful. At Confetti Cakes we always use the finest ingredients and make our cakes, cookies, and fillings from scratch — after all, the best part of a cake is how it tastes. These are some of our favorite recipes for cakes, fillings, and cookies, and are the perfect recipes to use. They taste amazing and they work perfectly, structure-wise, with the projects in this book.

When it comes to ingredients, **unsalted butter** is essential for the correct balance of flavor. It is also important to always use **whole milk** — the fat in it is necessary for proper baking chemistry. If you are trying to cut fat out of your diet eat a smaller piece of cake, but never use skim milk! Also, use **pure extracts** if you can find them.

We use the best chocolate for all of our creations. When our recipes call for cocoa, we use Valrhona chocolate. If you want kosher chocolate, try Scharffen Berger. If you can't find one of these brands, look for another dark-colored, 100 percent unsweetened cocoa. We also use the best quality semisweet (58 percent) chocolate blocks to chop for our ganache and melt for our chocolate and mocha buttercreams. The important thing to remember is not to use candy melts — they are not real chocolate.

Aside from using great ingredients, it is crucial to read through the entire recipe before you start so there are no surprises. Keep in mind that baking is similar to chemistry. Precise measurements are important (see conversion tables on page 218), so follow the recipes and the directions carefully, especially the ones in the recipe methods (for example, sifted, chopped, etc.). It is always best if your eggs and milk are at room temperature before mixing.

In most cases, you can use any cookie or cake and filling recipe in this section for the projects in this book, although occasionally we will suggest a flavor to use. However, when you are carving cake, you should always use a sturdy filling such as the Swiss-Meringue Buttercream or Ganache.

Chocolate Cake

**YIELD: THREE 9-INCH ROUNDS,
1 HALF SHEET (13 X 18 INCHES), 24 CUPCAKES**

What You Need

All-purpose flour	2⅔ cups (12 ounces)
Unsweetened cocoa powder	1¼ cups plus 2 tablespoons (4 ounces)
Baking powder	2 teaspoons
Baking soda	1 teaspoon
Salt	1 teaspoon
Sour cream	1 cup (8 ounces)
Pure vanilla extract	1 teaspoon
Pure almond extract	1 teaspoon
Unsalted butter	1 cup (2 sticks; 8 ounces)
Granulated sugar	2 cups (14 ounces)
Eggs	2
Strong coffee	1¼ cups (10 ounces)

This heavenly chocolate cake is our most requested and is the perfect treat for any chocoholic. The secret to making a great chocolate cake is using the best quality cocoa you can find. It really does make a difference.

Method

1.   Preheat the oven to 350°F. Brush the bottoms and sides of the pans with melted butter and line the bottoms with parchment paper.

2.   In a large bowl, sift together the flour, cocoa powder, baking powder, baking soda, and salt. Set aside.

3.   In a separate bowl, combine the sour cream, vanilla, and almond extract. Set aside.

4.   In the bowl of a standing mixer fitted with a paddle attachment, combine the butter and sugar and beat on medium speed until smooth.

5.   Set the mixer to low speed and add the eggs, one at a time, scraping thoroughly between each addition.

6.   Alternately add the flour and sour cream mixtures to the butter mixture in two batches, starting and ending with the flour mixture. Scrape down the bowl after each addition.

7.   Gradually pour in the coffee. Scrape down the bowl and beat until thoroughly combined.

8.   Divide the batter evenly between the cake pans or muffin tins. For 9-inch cake pans, bake 1 hour or until a toothpick comes out clean; for half-sheet pans, bake 45 minutes or until a toothpick comes out clean; for cupcakes, bake 20 to 25 minutes, or until they spring back after being touched.

9.   Allow the cakes to cool for 20 minutes. Once the cake is cool, release it from its pan by running a metal spatula or knife along the sides of the pan. Flip the cake over onto another pan or cake board and peel away the layer of parchment.

HOT TIP

■ Cakes can be stored in the freezer for up to five days, tightly wrapped in at least two layers of plastic wrap.

Vanilla Cake

This is a delicious white cake with a slightly crunchy top and is the perfect texture for creating sculpted cakes. The recipe calls only for egg whites, which makes it nice and light. Add extra flavor to this cake by brushing layers with flavored Simple Syrup (page 59) before filling and frosting.

YIELD: THREE 9-INCH ROUNDS,
1 HALF SHEET (13 X 18 INCHES), 24 CUPCAKES

What You Need

Cake flour	2 cups (8 ounces)
All-purpose flour	1¾ cups plus 1½ teaspoons (8 ounces)
Baking powder	2¼ teaspoons
Unsalted butter	1 cup (2 sticks; 8 ounces)
Granulated sugar	3 cups (21 ounces)
Salt	¾ teaspoon
Pure vanilla extract	1 tablespoon
Egg whites or pasteurized egg whites in liquid form	1 cup (8 ounces; about 7 eggs)
Milk	1½ cups (12 ounces)

Method

1.   Preheat the oven to 350°F. Brush the bottoms and sides of the pans with melted butter and line the bottoms with parchment paper.

2.   In a large bowl, sift together the cake flour, all-purpose flour, and baking powder. Set aside.

3.   In the bowl of a standing mixer fitted with a paddle attachment, combine the butter and sugar and beat on medium speed until light and fluffy.

4.   Add the salt and vanilla.

5.   Set the mixer to low speed and gradually add the egg whites, scraping often.

6.   Alternately add the flour mixture and milk to the butter mixture in two batches, starting with the flour. Scrape down the bowl between each addition and beat until thoroughly combined. Set the mixer to medium-high speed for about 20 seconds then stop and scrape the sides of the bowl.

7.   Divide the batter evenly between the cake pans or muffin tins. For 9-inch cake pans, bake 1 hour or until a toothpick comes out clean; for half-sheet pans, bake 45 minutes or until a toothpick comes out clean; for cupcakes, bake 20 to 25 minutes, or until they spring back after being touched.

8.   Allow the cake to cool for 20 minutes. Once the cake is cool, release it from its pan by running a metal spatula or knife along the sides of the pan. Flip the cake over onto another pan or cake board and peel away the layer of parchment.

Variation
To make this a **LEMON CAKE,** add the zest and juice of two lemons (about 1½ teaspoons of zest and 1 tablespoon of juice) to the batter in step 4.

HOT TIP
▪ Cakes can be stored in the freezer for up to five days, tightly wrapped in at least two layers of plastic wrap.

Red Velvet Cake

When I was searching for an extremely moist red velvet cake, my friend Jeri gave me this recipe to try. She is a fabulous baker, and this is one of her favorite recipes. In the South, red velvet cake, a cocoa and buttermilk-based cake, tinted red with food coloring, is traditionally paired with soft cream cheese frosting, but if you are making a sculpted cake, use the Swiss-Meringue Buttercream Frosting (page 56) as it is much more stable.

YIELD: THREE 9-INCH ROUNDS,
1 HALF SHEET (13 X 18 INCHES), 24 CUPCAKES

What You Need

Cake flour	3½ cups (14 ounces)
Unsweetened cocoa powder	½ cup (1½ ounces)
Salt	1½ teaspoons
Canola oil	2 cups (16 ounces)
Granulated sugar	2¼ cups plus 1 tablespoon (16 ounces)
Large eggs	3
Red food coloring	⅓ cup (3 ounces)
Pure vanilla extract	1½ teaspoons
Buttermilk	1¼ cup (10 ounces)
Baking soda	2 teaspoons
White vinegar	2½ teaspoons

Method

1.   Preheat the oven to 350°F. Brush the bottoms and sides of the pans with melted butter and line the bottoms with parchment paper.

2.   In a large bowl, sift together the cake flour, cocoa powder, and salt. Set aside.

3.   In the bowl of a standing mixer fitted with a paddle attachment, combine the oil and sugar and beat on medium speed until incorporated.

4.   Set the mixer to low speed and add the eggs, one at a time, scraping thoroughly between each addition.

5.   Add the red food coloring and vanilla in a slow stream and beat until incorporated.

6.   Alternately add the flour mixture and buttermilk in two batches, starting with the flour. Scrape down the bowl between each addition and beat until thoroughly combined.

7.   In a small bowl, whisk together the baking soda and vinegar. Set the mixer to medium speed. Immediately add the baking soda mixture and beat for 10 seconds.

8.   Divide the batter evenly between the cake pans or muffin tins. For 9-inch cake pans, bake 1 hour or until a toothpick comes out clean; for half-sheet pans, bake 45 minutes or until a toothpick comes out clean; for cupcakes, bake 20 to 25 minutes, or until they spring back after being touched.

9.   Allow the cake to cool for 20 minutes. Once the cake is cool, release it from its pan by running a metal spatula or knife along the sides of the pan. Flip the cake over onto another pan or cake board and peel away the layer of parchment.

HOT TIP

■ Cakes can be stored in the freezer for up to five days, tightly wrapped in at least two layers of plastic wrap.

Banana Cake

Imagine the most divine banana bread you have ever tasted in the form of an extremely moist and flavorful cake. This is it! It's the best banana cake recipe we've ever tried.

**YIELD: THREE 9-INCH ROUNDS,
1 HALF SHEET (13 X 18 INCHES), 24 CUPCAKES**

What You Need

Baking soda	2 teaspoons
All-purpose flour	3¼ cup plus 1½ tablespoons (15 ounces)
Unsalted butter	1 cup (2 sticks; 8 ounces)
Granulated sugar	2½ cups (17½ ounces)
Large eggs	4
Sour cream	1 cup (8 ounces)
Pure vanilla extract	1 tablespoon
Very ripe bananas	6

Method

1.   Preheat the oven to 350°F. Brush the bottoms and sides of the pans with melted butter and line the bottoms with parchment paper.

2.   In a large bowl, sift together the baking soda and flour. Set aside.

3.   Peel the bananas and mash them in a bowl. Set aside.

4.   In the bowl of a standing mixer fitted with a paddle attachment, combine the butter and sugar and beat on medium speed until smooth.

5.   Set the mixer to low speed and add the eggs, one at a time, scraping thoroughly between each addition.

6.   Add the sour cream and vanilla and beat until thoroughly combined.

7.   Add the flour mixture in two batches, scraping down the bowl after each addition.

8.   Add the bananas and beat until just combined. Do not overmix.

9.   Divide the batter evenly between the cake pans or muffin tins. For 9-inch cake pans, bake 1 hour or until a toothpick comes out clean; for half-sheet pans, bake 45 minutes or until a toothpick comes out clean; for cupcakes, bake 20 to 25 minutes, or until they spring back after being touched.

10.   Allow the cake to cool for 20 minutes. Once the cake is cool, release it from its pan by running a metal spatula or knife along the sides of the pan. Flip the cake over onto another pan or cake board and peel away the layer of parchment.

HOT TIPS

▪ Banana cake tastes best when it has had time to rest and develop its flavors. For best results, bake the cake at least one day in advance and let it rest in the refrigerator, wrapped in plastic, before splitting and filling.

▪ Cakes can be stored in the freezer for up to five days if tightly wrapped in at least two layers of plastic wrap.

Vanilla Sugar Cookies

This delicious cookie recipe comes from my grandmomi Pearl. She would make them for me after musical recitals and on special occasions. These buttery cookies are perfect to bake in shapes and then decorate. To maintain their shape, it is important to freeze the cut cookies for at least 15 minutes before you bake them. (Feel free to double this recipe.)

YIELD: APPROXIMATELY 12 3-INCH COOKIES, DEPENDING ON SIZE OF COOKIE CUTTERS

What You Need

All-purpose flour	4⅓ cups plus 2 tablespoons (20 ounces)
Salt	1 teaspoon
Baking powder	1 teaspoon
Unsalted butter	¾ cup (1½ sticks; 6 ounces)
Granulated sugar	½ cup plus 2 tablespoons (4 ounces)
Large egg	1
Pure vanilla extract	1 teaspoon

Method

1. In a medium bowl, sift together the flour, salt, and baking powder. Set aside.

2. In the bowl of a standing mixer fitted with a paddle attachment, combine the butter and sugar and beat on medium speed until light and fluffy. Add the egg and vanilla and beat until combined.

3. Add the flour mixture in 2 batches, scraping down the bowl after each addition. Beat until the dough just comes together, being careful not to overmix.

4. Turn out the dough onto a lightly floured surface. Form the dough into a ball, wrap it in plastic, and refrigerate for 30 minutes.

5. Place the ball of dough between two pieces of parchment paper and roll out to ¼ inch thick. Keeping the dough in the parchment, transfer to a cookie sheet and place in the refrigerator for at least 1 hour.

6. Preheat the oven to 350°F.

7. Cut out the cookies in the desired shapes and place on a half-sheet pan lined with parchment paper or an ungreased nonstick cookie sheet, at least 1 inch apart. Transfer to the freezer and chill for at least 15 minutes or until they are stiff.

8. Bake until the cookies are light golden brown, about 10 minutes.

9. Let cookies cool completely on the sheets before decorating. (They will still be soft when they come out of the oven and may break or become misshapen if they are moved off the sheets before cool.)

Variations

CITRUS COOKIES: Add 1 teaspoon of finely grated lemon or orange zest to the butter and sugar mixture in step 1.

ALMOND COOKIES: Replace the vanilla with 1 teaspoon of pure almond extract.

HOT TIP

■ This dough can be made up to 2 weeks ahead of time. Roll out the dough between two pieces of parchment paper, wrap in plastic, and freeze. Defrost until the dough is pliable enough to cut, about 10–15 minutes. Continue from step 6.

Chocolate Cookies

This is a light and crisp chocolate sugar cookie.
It is important to use the best quality bittersweet chocolate you can find. If you have trouble finding bittersweet chocolate, you can use semisweet chocolate instead.

YIELD: APPROXIMATELY 12 3-INCH COOKIES, DEPENDING ON SIZE OF COOKIE CUTTERS

What You Need

All-purpose flour	2⅓ cups plus 2 tablespoons (11 ounces)
Salt	¼ teaspoon
Baking soda	½ teaspoon
Bittersweet chocolate, chopped or morsels	6 ounces
Unsalted butter	1 cup (2 sticks; 8 ounces)
Granulated sugar	1¼ cups plus 4 tablespoons (8 ounces)
Large egg	1
Pure vanilla extract	1 teaspoon

Method

1.   In a medium bowl, sift together the flour, salt, and baking soda. Set aside.

2.   Place the chocolate in a double boiler and melt over medium heat. Alternately, place the chocolate in a bowl and microwave in 15-second increments, stirring between each increment. Be careful not to let the chocolate burn.

3.   In the bowl of a standing mixer fitted with a paddle attachment, combine the butter and sugar and beat on medium speed until light and fluffy. Add the egg and vanilla and beat until combined.

4.   Set the mixer to low speed and add the melted chocolate.

5.   Add the flour mixture in 2 batches, scraping down the bowl after each addition. Beat until the dough just comes together, being careful not to overmix.

6.   Turn out the dough onto a lightly floured surface. Form the dough into a ball, wrap it in plastic, and refrigerate for 30 minutes.

7.   Place the dough between two pieces of parchment paper and roll out to ⅛ inch thick. Transfer the dough to the refrigerator and chill for at least 1 hour.

8.   Preheat the oven to 350°F.

9.   Cut out the cookies in the desired shapes and place on a half-sheet pan lined with parchment paper or an ungreased nonstick cookie sheet, at least 1 inch apart. Transfer to the refrigerator and chill for at least 15 minutes or until they are stiff.

10. Bake until the cookies are slightly firm to the touch, about 10 minutes.

11. Let cookies cool completely before decorating.

HOT TIP

■ This dough can be made up to 2 weeks ahead of time. Roll out the dough between two pieces of parchment paper, wrap in plastic and freeze. Defrost until the dough is pliable enough to cut, about 10–15 minutes. Continue from step 8.

Cupcake Frosting

This is the sweetest frosting around, and it is perfect for delicious cupcakes. Kids and adults with any kind of sweet tooth crave this frosting. I do not recommend it for filling any of the sculpted cakes, because it lacks the structure needed to make the cakes stable.

YIELD: FROSTING FOR 24 CUPCAKES

What You Need

Unsalted butter	1 cup (2 sticks; 8 ounces)
Confectioners' sugar	8 cups (28 ounces)
Milk	½ cup (4 ounces)
Pure vanilla extract	2 teaspoons

Method

1. In the bowl of a mixer fitted with a paddle attachment, beat the butter on medium speed until smooth.

2. Turn the mixer to low speed and add 1 cup of the confectioners' sugar and beat until combined. Scrape the bowl thoroughly.

3. In a small bowl, combine the milk and the vanilla. Add to the butter-sugar mixture. Set the mixer to medium speed and beat until light and fluffy.

4. Gradually add the remaining confectioners' sugar, adding as much as you need to achieve a smooth and stiff consistency.

5. Use immediately, store in an airtight container at room temperature for up to 2 days, or refrigerate for up to 10 days.

Swiss-Meringue Buttercream

This is the world's greatest and most versatile buttercream. It is incredibly smooth and not too sweet, and you can add just about any flavoring to it. It is also a nice, stable filling — perfect for sculpted and tiered cakes.

YIELD: 8 CUPS (ENOUGH TO FILL AND CRUMB COAT TWO 9-INCH ROUND CAKES, EACH CONSISTING OF TWO LAYERS OF FILLING AND THREE LAYERS OF CAKE; OR 24 CUPCAKES WITH SWIRLS)

What You Need

Granulated sugar	2¾ cups plus 3 tablespoons (20 ounces)
Egg whites, or pasteurized egg whites in liquid form	1¼ cups (10 ounces)
Unsalted butter, cubed and softened	2½ cups (5 sticks; 20 ounces)
Pure vanilla extract	¼ cup plus 2 tablespoons (2½ ounces)

Method

1. In the bowl of a standing mixer, thoroughly whisk together sugar and egg whites.

2. Set the bowl over a pot of boiling water. Whisking constantly, heat the mixture until all the sugar crystals have dissolved and the mixture is hot. Get it as hot as you can but be careful not to cook the eggs.

3. Put the bowl back in the mixer fitted with a whip attachment. Beat on high speed until the mixture forms a stiff meringue and the bottom of the bowl comes to room temperature, about 10 minutes.

4. Stop the mixer and replace the whip attachment with the paddle attachment.

5. Set the mixer to low speed and add the butter, a few cubes at a time. When all the butter is incorporated, turn the mixer to medium speed and beat until fluffy.

6. Set the mixer to low speed and add the vanilla. Once the vanilla is incorporated, scrape the bowl and continue to mix on medium speed until you have a smooth, creamy texture. If the buttercream is too liquid, refrigerate until completely cool and stiff, then rewhip.

7. You can use the buttercream immediately, store it in an airtight container at room temperature for up to two days, or refrigerate it in an airtight container for ten days.

Variations

Add the ingredients for these variations after step 6 in the original recipe. Be sure that the buttercream is cool and stiff before adding any variations.

CHOCOLATE: Add ½ cup (4 ounces) of melted semisweet (58 percent) chocolate in a steady stream while mixing on low speed. Be sure that the chocolate is cool or it will melt the buttercream.

PRALINE: Add ½ cup (4 ounces) of praline paste in small additions on low speed. Once incorporated, turn your mixer to high speed for one minute.

MOCHA: Add ¼ cup (2 ounces) of cold strong coffee and ¼ cup melted and cooled semisweet (58 percent) chocolate (2 ounces), each in a slow steady stream while mixing on low speed.

RASPBERRY: Add ½ cup (4 ounces) of seedless raspberry puree.

CREAM CHEESE: Add 1 cup (8 ounces) softened cream cheese.

HOT TIPS

Before you begin this recipe, clean all utensils and equipment thoroughly with a paper towel moistened with lemon juice. This eliminates any grease or oil that may prevent the meringue from whipping to its proper volume and consistency.

After you refrigerate the buttercream, you need to reconstitute it before you can use it. Heat ⅓ of your buttercream in the microwave until it is warm to the touch. Place the remaining ⅔ in the bowl of a mixer and beat on medium speed. Add the warmed buttercream and beat until it is creamy.

Chocolate Ganache

Chocolate ganache is a decadent cake filling or frosting similar to the fudgy inside of a chocolate truffle. When made properly, it is smooth and creamy. You can adjust the thickness by changing the proportion of cream to chocolate. Always use the best quality chocolate you can.

YIELD: 4 CUPS (ENOUGH TO FILL ONE 9-INCH ROUND CAKE CONSISTING OF TWO LAYERS OF FILLING AND THREE LAYERS OF CAKE)

What You Need

Bittersweet chocolate, chopped	16 ounces
Heavy cream	1 cup (8 ounces)

Method

1.   Place the chocolate in a metal or ovenproof glass bowl. Set aside.

2.   Heat the cream in a saucepan over medium-high heat, stirring frequently, until it starts to boil. Be careful because cream boils quickly and can boil over if you leave it for a few seconds.

3.   Remove the cream from the heat immediately and pour over the chocolate. Let the mixture stand for 2 to 3 minutes.

4.   Gently stir the mixture with a whisk until the chocolate is completely melted and there are no noticeable traces of cream.

5.   Allow the ganache to sit at room temperature to cool and thicken.

6.   When the ganache is cool, store it in an airtight container. Ganache can be kept for 2 days at room temperature or for 10 days refrigerated.

HOT TIP

■ To reconstitute refrigerated ganache, heat it in a double boiler over very low heat to prevent burning. Heating gently makes it easier to control the consistency of the ganache for filling a cake.

Royal Icing

Royal Icing is a key element for any cookie or cake decorator. It is the sweet, edible "glue" that is used to hold together or attach finished tiers of cake, ice cookies, create decorations, and attach decorations directly onto the cake. The stiffness of the icing is determined by the amount of sugar used. If you need a stiffer icing add more sugar; if you need a looser icing for flood work, add a few drops of water until you achieve the consistency desired.

YIELD: 4½ CUPS

What You Need

Pasteurized egg whites	⅓ cup (3 ounces)
Sifted confectioners' sugar	4½ cups plus 1 tablespoon (16 ounces)
Lemon juice	½ teaspoon

Method

1. In the bowl of an electric mixer fitted with a paddle attachment, beat the egg whites on medium speed until soft peaks form.

2. Gradually add the confectioners' sugar, ½ cup (4 ounces) at a time, on medium-low speed. Scrape down the bowl thoroughly between each addition.

3. Add the lemon juice and beat on medium-high speed until stiff peaks form and the icing is no longer shiny, 6 to 8 minutes.

4. Use immediately or place the icing into an airtight container. You can keep Royal Icing in the refrigerator for up to five days.

HOT TIPS

■ Allow Royal Icing to come to room temperature before you use it. It will be much easier to mix and pipe.

■ If you are making this for someone who might be allergic to eggs, use a mixture of 2 tablespoons plus 2 teaspoons (1½ ounces) meringue powder and ½ cup (4 ounces) water to replace the egg whites. Follow the rest of the recipe as above.

Simple Syrup

Simple syrup is a fabulous way to add a delicious hint of flavor to your cake — and to keep it incredibly moist. This recipe is a foundation for a nice, sweet syrup. Once it has cooled, you can add citrus juices, liquors, or extracts to complement the flavor of your cake. We love to brush flavored simple syrup on each layer of vanilla cake before filling the cake with buttercream.

YIELD: 2 CUPS

What You Need

Granulated sugar	1 cup (7 ounces)
Water	1 cup (8 ounces)

Method

1. Combine the sugar and water in a medium saucepan. Stir with a whisk to hydrate the sugar completely. Without stirring, bring to a boil over high heat.

2. When the syrup comes to a boil, remove it from the heat and allow to cool.

3. When cool, simple syrup can be stored in an airtight container in the refrigerator for up to two weeks.

4. To use, simply brush on the top layers of cake before placing the filling.

HOT TIP

■ If you want to **add flavors to this basic simple syrup,** the amount of flavor you should add depends on how strong you would like the syrup to be. About ¼ cup (2 ounces) is a good start.

Servings

The following chart will help you to determine **how much cake you need** to serve a specific number of people. See below for the number of servings per size and shape of cake.

SIZE	ROUND CAKES	SQUARE CAKES
6-inch	6	10
8-inch	18	25
10-inch	30	40
12-inch	45	50
14-inch	60	75
16-inch	80	100

Rolled Fondant

At Confetti Cakes, we buy fondant by the tub. I find prefabricated fondant has a higher quality and usually a finer taste than what you could make at home. You can find premade fondant in many flavors; our favorites include chocolate and vanilla (see Resources). You can also find kosher rolled fondant. If you cannot find rolled fondant in a store near you or you would like to experiment with a recipe at home, this is the one to use.

YIELD: 2 POUNDS (ENOUGH TO COVER ONE 10-INCH ROUND, 4-INCH-HIGH CAKE)

What You Need

Confectioners' sugar, sifted	9 cups plus 2 tablespoons (32 ounces)
Cold water	3 tablespoons
Unflavored gelatin	1 tablespoon
Light corn syrup	½ cup (4 ounces)
Glycerin	1½ tablespoons
Pure vanilla extract	1 tablespoon

Method

1. Place 6 cups of the confectioners' sugar in the bowl of an electric mixer fitted with a paddle attachment.

2. In a small bowl combine the cold water and gelatin. Allow the mixture to sit for 2 minutes.

3. Place the gelatin mixture in a double boiler and melt over low heat. Remove from heat and stir in the corn syrup, glycerin, and vanilla.

4. With the mixer on low speed, pour the gelatin mixture into the confectioners' sugar. Turn the mixer to medium speed and beat until a sticky ball forms.

5. Using a spatula coated in shortening, scrape the dough onto a clean surface and knead in the remaining confectioners' sugar until the fondant is smooth.

6. Wrap the fondant in several layers of plastic and store at room temperature for at least 24 hours in an airtight container before using.

HOT TIPS

▥ Do not get rolled fondant wet. It gets sticky and becomes difficult to use.

▥ In hot climates or in the summer you may need to use a little extra confectioners' sugar. If possible, work in an air-conditioned area.

▥ A fondant-covered cake will keep for two days without refrigeration. Store it in a cool and dry area.

▥ For flavor variations, substitute 1 tablespoon of another extract such as almond, lemon, or mint for the vanilla.

How Much Fondant?

This chart helps you determine approximately **how much fondant you need** to cover cakes that are 4 inches high. If you are using fondant for the first time or you are a beginner, start off using more fondant than called for — it is easier to learn with too much fondant than too little.

ROUND CAKES	SQUARE CAKES
4-inch: ¾ pound	**4-inch:** 1 pound
6-inch: 1 pound	**6-inch:** 1½ pounds
8-inch: 1½ pounds	**8-inch:** 2 pounds
10-inch: 2 pounds	**10-inch:** 3 pounds
12-inch: 3 pounds	**12-inch:** 4 pounds
14-inch: 4 pounds	**14-inch:** 5 pounds
16-inch: 5 pounds	**16-inch:** 6 pounds

Measuring Gum Paste and Fondant Without a Scale

If you do not have a scale, use this chart to approximate the amount needed.

¼ ounce — small marble
½ ounce — large gumball
1 ounce — golf ball
4 ounces — racquet ball
6 ounces — tennis ball
8 ounces — orange

Cookies

Cookies

Cookies are a great way to get started in pastry decoration, and you can make them for just about any occasion. We hope you will use the projects in this chapter as inspiration to create your own special cookies. You can use a simple vanilla or chocolate cookie dough as your base, cut out any shape imaginable using a cookie cutter or a template you create yourself, and decorate them using the techniques in this book.

If you are making a large quantity of cookies, I recommend making everything in two stages by splitting the baking and the decorating into at least two days. Make all the dough at once and roll it out between sheets of parchment paper. Cut out all the cookies and transfer them to baking sheets. (If you do not have enough baking sheets, cut out the cookies and keep them on the parchment paper so they are ready to be transferred onto the cookie sheets.) Freeze the cookies in batches and pop them in the oven once they are firm. Keep rotating the trays between the freezer and the oven until they are all baked.

Once the cookies are cool, wrap them in plastic overnight and prepare your Royal Icing, fondant, and gum-paste colors. If your cookies require sugar decorations that need to dry ahead of time, make them before making the other decorative elements.

Heart Cookies

YIELD: APPROXIMATELY 24 COOKIES

These cookies say **"I LOVE YOU!"** Make them for your favorite girl or guy, or your best friend. They are ideal on Valentine's Day in shades of red, pink, and white, and sweet any other time of year, too — you can make them in all kinds of colors. We love to make an assortment of vanilla and chocolate cookies decorated with Royal Icing and sanding sugar.

Method

1.   Prepare the cookie dough and roll it out as directed. Use a heart cutter to cut out cookies and bake according to the recipe. While the cookies are cooling, prepare the Royal Icing.

2.   Divide the Royal Icing into 4 portions, and dye one pale pink, one medium pink, and one red. Leave the last portion white. Fill a piping bag fitted with a #2 tip and, using the shape of the cookie as your guide, outline the cookies in white, pale pink, medium pink, and red (or whatever combination of colors you plan to use).

3.   Add water to the remaining icing to loosen and fill a pastry bag fitted with a #3 tip. Flood cookies one at a time. Hold the flooded cookie over a bowl and spoon on the sanding sugar. (You will need about 3 tablespoons of sanding sugar per cookie.) Let the cookie dry for at least 20 minutes before removing the excess sugar. If you disturb the cookie too soon the icing may spill out of the sides.

HOT TIPS

▮ Mix and match the colored icings and sugars to get various effects. The light pink sanding sugar looks very different on a cookie filled with white icing than it does on a cookie filled with red icing.

▮ For a different taste, forgo the icing, spread the cookies with raspberry preserves, and use it as the "glue" for sanding sugar.

What You Need

COOKIES

1 recipe cookie dough
(see *Basic Recipes* pages 53–54)

1 recipe Royal Icing (page 58)

MATERIALS

Food-coloring gels: rose pink, electric pink, and super red

Sanding sugar in various colors

EQUIPMENT

2½-inch heart cookie cutter

Pastry bags and plastic couplers

Pastry tips: #2, #3

Scissors

X-acto knife

Toothpicks

Small bowls

Spoon(s)

TECHNIQUES

Dyeing Royal Icing (page 40)

Filling a pastry bag (page 38)

Flooding (page 25)

Decorating with sanding sugar (page 27)

Snowflake Cookies

YIELD: APPROXIMATELY 12 COOKIES

What You Need

COOKIES

1 recipe Chocolate Cookie dough (page 54)

½ recipe Royal Icing (page 58)

MATERIALS

White sanding sugar (optional)

EQUIPMENT

Snowflake cookie cutters
(cutter sizes: 4 inches, 2½ inches)

Pastry bag and plastic coupler

#2 pastry tip

Scissors

Toothpicks

TECHNIQUES

Filling a pastry bag (page 38)

Piping dots and straight lines (page 39)

What could be better than chocolate snowflakes on a cold winter night? These make beautiful gifts, too. Package each cookie in a cellophane bag tied with a ribbon, and give them as edible ornaments. The dark chocolate cookies with the white Royal Icing are striking and graphic—
and they taste delicious!

Method

1.   Prepare the cookie dough and roll it out as directed. Use a snowflake cutter to cut out cookies and bake according to the recipe. While the cookies are cooling, prepare the Royal Icing.

2.   Fill a pastry bag fitted with a #2 tip with stiff white Royal Icing.

3.   Create designs on your cooled cookies with a series of straight lines and dots. I think symmetrical designs look best on these. Real snowflakes are all one-of-a-kind, so make up your own patterns. Use toothpicks to fix any piping mistakes.

HOT TIP
■ For an added wintry effect, display your cookies on a tray of white sanding sugar.

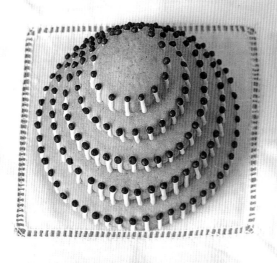

Stacked Wedding
Cake Cookies

YIELD: APPROXIMATELY 5 TIERED CAKE COOKIES

I am a cookie addict, so I love the idea of making something from tiers of cookies that looks like a cake. These are precious as dessert or favors for a bridal shower, wedding, or afternoon tea. Serve them on cute little napkins or lace doilies on plates. Or use flattened cupcake wrappers — if you use fluted cutters, the pleats on the cookies will match the pleats on the wrappers. Start at least 1 day in advance if you want to decorate these cookies with sugar flowers. Otherwise, you can start and finish them the same day.

Method

MAKE THE SUGAR FLOWERS (OPTIONAL) ONE DAY IN ADVANCE

1.   Take about ½ ounce (a large gumball) per cookie of fondant and roll it out to 1⁄16 inch thick on a smooth surface greased with shortening. Cut out two sizes of flowers using the 5-petal cutters. Lay them in an egg carton to keep the petals from drying flat. Let dry overnight.

2.   Prepare the cookie dough and roll it out to ⅜ inch thick. Cut out at least 4 cookies with each size cutter. Bake as directed in the recipe. Let cookies cool completely.

3.   While the cookies are cooling, prepare the Royal Icing and put a small amount in a pastry bag fitted with the #2 tip.

4.   When the cookies are cool, glue them together with dots of icing about the size of a dime. Use four or five cookies per "cake," depending on how high you want the stacks to be.

5.   Dye the remaining icing in whatever colors you choose and, using a pastry bag fitted with a #2 tip, pipe dots, straight lines, and swags on the outside edges of the cookies.

6.   Once the cookies are dry, if you made sugar flowers, attach them to the edges of the cookies with tiny dots of icing. Apply small dots of pink icing to decorate the centers of the flowers.

HOT TIPS

■ Instead of piping exact designs, use an assortment of decorations. Add edible pearls or dragées along the cookies' edges or dust the cookies with confectioners' sugar or sanding sugar.

■ Add a layer of preserves between each layer to give a delicious flavor accent.

■ You can use this idea for brownies, too. Prepare a pan of ½-inch-thick brownies, cut out circles using different sized cutters, and stack them together with frosting, icing, or preserves.

What You Need

COOKIES

1 recipe cookie dough
(see *Basic Recipes* pages 53–54)

½ recipe Royal Icing (page 58)

MATERIALS

2 ounces gum paste or fondant
(store-bought or page 60) (for flowers)

Shortening (for flowers)

Food-coloring gels: rose pink, violet, buckeye brown

EQUIPMENT

2 sizes (small and mini) 5-petal flower cutters (for flowers)

Egg cartons (for drying flowers)

Fluted or plain round cookie cutters (cutter sizes: 1 inch, 1½ inch, 2 inches, 2½ inches, 3 inches)

Toothpicks

Pastry bags and plastic couplers

Scissors

Pastry tips: #1, #2

TECHNIQUES

Filling a pastry bag (page 38)

Dyeing Royal Icing (page 40)

Piping dots, straight lines, and swags (page 39)

Baby Onesie Cookies

YIELD: APPROXIMATELY 12 COOKIES

What You Need

COOKIES

1 recipe Vanilla Sugar Cookie dough (page 53)

1 recipe Royal Icing (page 58)

MATERIALS

2 ounces gum paste or fondant (store-bought or page 60)

Shortening (for rolling out fondant or gum paste)

Food-coloring gels: super red, lemon yellow, royal blue, leaf green, coal black

EQUIPMENT

3¾-inch by 4¼-inch onesie cookie cutter or template (page 90)

Pastry bags and plastic couplers

Pastry tips: #2, #3

¾-inch heart cutter

¾-inch star cutter

Scissors

X-acto knife

Plastic mat

Small rolling pin

1 small paintbrush

1 small dish of water

Toothpicks

TECHNIQUES

Making a template (page 27)

Dyeing Royal Icing (page 40)

Filling a pastry bag (page 38)

Flooding (page 25)

Overpiping (page 26)

Dyeing fondant and gum paste (page 40)

These are **adorable for a baby shower** or to welcome home a brand-new baby. Play around with the decorations — we have several delightful ideas here, or you could write the name or the birth date of the baby or make up your own cute terms of endearment.

Method

1. Prepare the cookie dough and roll it out as directed. Use the onesie cutter or template to cut out cookies. Bake as directed in the recipe. Let cookies cool completely. While the cookies are cooling, prepare the Royal Icing.

2. Divide the Royal Icing into 3 portions and dye one pale blue and one pale green. Leave one portion white. Put each color in a pastry bag fitted with a #2 tip and outline the cookies.

3. Add water to the remaining icing and fill the loose icing in a pastry bag fitted with a #3 tip. Flood the cookies in white, pale blue, and pale green. Let the cookies dry, uncovered, on a flat surface for at least 3 hours.

4. Using the same colors of stiff icing you used to outline the cookies, with a #2 tip, overpipe the original outline, plus the neckline, the shoulders, and the leg openings.

5. Divide the fondant into 4 portions and dye each red, yellow, and black, leaving 1 portion white. On a smooth surface greased with shortening, roll out the red and yellow fondants to about 1/16 inch thick. Cut out red heart and yellow star shapes using the small cutters. Attach the shapes to the onesies, just above the center, with a dab of water or Royal Icing.

6. To make the sheep decoration, roll a small ball of white fondant or gum paste. Scrunching with your fingers, make indentations to look like sheep's wool. Attach it just above the middle of the onesie. Using a tiny piece of black fondant or gum paste form 4 tiny balls for the sheep's face, feet, and tail. Attach them with a dab of water.

Birthday Cake Cookies

YIELD: APPROXIMATELY 12 COOKIES

Most people think the only dessert to have at a birthday party is cake. What about fun cookies in the shape of birthday cakes? These make great party favors, too, and you can decorate them in so many ways. You can follow the designs pictured here, or use them as inspiration to create your own designs. Pick your favorite and make all cookies in the same design, or choose a variety of designs.

What You Need

COOKIES

1 recipe cookie dough (see *Basic Recipes* pages 53–54)

1 recipe Royal Icing (page 58)

MATERIALS

2 ounces gum paste (for flowers)

Shortening (for flowers)

Food-coloring gels: rose pink, electric pink, lemon yellow, sunset orange, leaf green, super red, sky blue, royal blue

Sanding sugars (optional)

EQUIPMENT

Plastic mat

Small rolling pin

Small 5-petal cutter (for flowers)

Paper towels or egg carton

3½ x 4½-inch tiered cake cookie cutter or template (page 90)

Toothpicks

Pastry bags and plastic couplers

Pastry tips: #1, #2, #3, #4, #10

Scissors

TECHNIQUES

Making a template (page 27)

Dyeing Royal Icing (page 40)

Filling a pastry bag (page 38)

Flooding and drop-in flooding (pages 25–26)

Piping dots and straight lines (page 39)

Decorating with sanding sugar (page 27)

Method

ONE DAY IN ADVANCE: MAKE THE SUGAR FLOWERS (OPTIONAL)

1.   On a smooth surface greased with shortening, roll out a piece of gum paste or fondant the size of a large marble to ¹⁄₁₆ inch thick. Cut out 8 flowers using the 5-petal cutter. Lay them on a crumpled paper towel or in an egg carton to keep the petals from drying flat. Let dry overnight.

2.   Prepare the cookie dough and roll it out as directed. Use the tiered cake cookie cutter or template to cut out cookies. Bake as directed in the recipe. Let cookies cool completely. While they are cooling, prepare the Royal Icing.

3.   Divide the icing and dye each portion with the colors you will use. For each color make half stiff Royal Icing and half loose icing. Put the stiff icing in a pastry bag fitted with the #2 tip and the loose icing in a bag fitted with a #3 tip.

4.   Pipe a complete outline on the bottom two tiers with stiff icing. If you are using different colors for each tier, pipe a horizontal line to divide the two tiers and prevent icing from spilling over. (Leave the top tier empty; this is where you will pipe the birthday cake candles.) Starting in the center of each tier, flood each tier with the corresponding color of loose icing.

5.   For cookies getting sanding sugar, hold the flooded cookie over a bowl and spoon on the sanding sugar (you need about 3 tablespoons per cookie). Let the cookies dry for at least 20 minutes before removing the excess sugar. If you disturb the cookie too soon the icing may spill out of the sides.

6.   For the candles, fill a pastry bag fitted with a #1 tip with stiff Royal Icing, using whatever color you wish, and pipe four straight, vertical lines on the top tier of the cookie. Fill a pastry bag fitted with a #1 tip with yellow icing and use it to pipe dots for the candle flames.

7.   Once the cookies are dry, if you made sugar flowers, attach them with tiny dabs of Royal Icing. Pipe centers onto the flowers using the same yellow icing you used for the candle flames.

Techniques for Cookies Pictured (clockwise from top right)

PALE PINK: Piped dots in stiff Royal Icing (#1 tip); gum-paste or fondant polka dots made with the top of a #10 tip and attached with a tiny dab of Royal Icing.

WHITE CONFETTI: Drop-in flooding in various colors in a random pattern, applying more or less pressure to vary the size of the dots.

DAISY: Sanding sugar coat, fondant or gum-paste flowers attached with tiny dabs of Royal Icing.

BLUE AND WHITE: Bottom tier: lines and dots in stiff Royal Icing (#1 tip). Second tier: dots in Royal Icing (#4 tip for pink, #1 tip for orange). Border: Piping dots in Royal Icing (#1 tip).

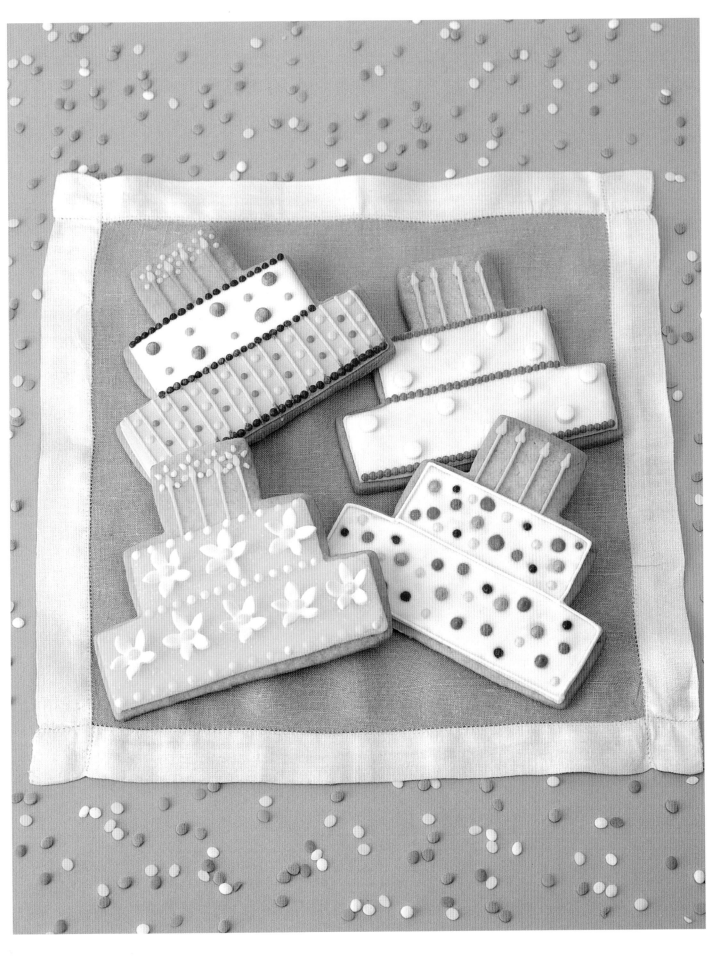

Stiletto Cookies

YIELD: APPROXIMATELY 12 COOKIES

These cookies can be as sexy (or as sweet) as your favorite pair of stiletto heels. **Dress them up with flowers, sassy patterns,** and your favorite colors. Make them pretty with tiny bows or polka dots, too.

Method

ONE DAY IN ADVANCE: MAKE THE SUGAR FLOWERS (OPTIONAL)

1. For the flowers: Dye the gum paste or fondant the colors desired. On a smooth surface greased with shortening, roll out a piece of gum paste the size of a large marble to $1/16$ inch thick. Cut out flowers using the 5-petal cutter. Lay them on a crumpled paper towel or in an egg carton to keep the petals from drying flat. Let dry overnight. For the bows, see page 44.

2. Prepare the cookie dough and roll it out as directed. Use a shoe cookie cutter or template to cut out cookies. Bake as directed in the recipe. Let cookies cool completely. While they are cooling, prepare the Royal Icing.

3. Divide the icing and dye each portion with the colors you will use. For each color make stiff icing and loose icing. Put the stiff icing in a pastry bag fitted with the #2 tip and the loose icing in a bag fitted with a #3 tip.

4. Outline and flood the cookies in your desired colors, leaving about $1/8$ inch at the bottom of each shoe's heel for a "leather" fondant heel.

5. For cookies getting sanding sugar, hold the flooded cookie over a bowl and spoon on the sanding sugar (you need about 3 tablespoons of sanding sugar per cookie). Let the cookies dry, uncovered, on a flat surface for at least 20 minutes before removing excess sugar.

6. To make the heel tap, dye fondant or gum paste brown, roll out a small piece, cut out a tiny rectangle about $1/8$ x $3/8$ inch, and attach it to the bottom of the cookie's heel with a tiny dab of water.

7. Once the cookies are dry, if you made sugar flowers or bows, attach them with tiny dabs of icing. Pipe centers onto the flowers using red icing and a #2 tip.

Techniques for Cookies Pictured

CHOCOLATE BROWN: Outline and flood in icing, bow and stitching piped in Royal Icing (#2 tip).

RUBY SLIPPERS: Outline and flood in icing, then coat with sanding sugar. Fondant or gum-paste bow attached with a dab of icing.

PINK LADY: Outline and flood in icing, pipe dots in icing (#2 tip).

SPARKLY PINK: Outline and flood in icing, then coat with sanding sugar. Bow in icing (#2 tip).

POLKA DOTS: Outline and flood in icing, pipe dots in Royal Icing (#2 tip).

FLOWER POWER: Outline and flood in icing, then coat with sanding sugar. Gum-paste flower attached with a tiny dab of icing.

GREEN WITH ENVY: Outline and flood in icing. Fondant or gum-paste shoe strap attached with dab of icing. Stitching piped in icing (#2 tip).

What You Need

COOKIES

1 recipe cookie dough (see *Basic Recipes* pages 53–54)

1 recipe Royal Icing (page 58)

MATERIALS

2 ounces gum paste or fondant (store-bought or on page 60)

Shortening for flowers (optional)

Food-coloring gels: rose pink, electric pink, lemon yellow, buckeye brown, sunset orange, leaf green, super red, sky blue, coal black

Sanding sugars (optional)

EQUIPMENT

Plastic mat

Small rolling pin

5-petal cutter (for flowers)

Paper towels or egg carton (for flowers)

5 x $3½$-inch shoe cookie cutter or template (page 90)

Toothpicks

Pastry bags and plastic couplers

Pastry tips: #2, #3

Scissors

TECHNIQUES

Making a template (page 27)

Dyeing Royal Icing (page 40)

Filling a pastry bag (page 38)

Flooding (page 25)

Piping dots and straight lines (page 39)

Dyeing fondant and gum paste (page 40)

Decorating with sanding sugar (page 27)

Making sugar bows and ribbons (page 44)

Handbag Cookies

YIELD: APPROXIMATELY 12 COOKIES

I love bags of all shapes, sizes, and colors. Making handbag cookies is the best way to have all my favorites without breaking the bank! These cookies are perfect for Mother's Day, a fashionista's birthday party, or a bridal shower. The dark chocolate cookie background allows the colors and patterns to pop — but you can make great-looking handbags from vanilla cookies, too.

Method

1. Prepare the cookie dough and roll it out as directed in the recipe. Use the handbag cookie cutter or a template to cut out cookies. Bake as directed in the recipe. Let cookies cool completely. While they are cooling, prepare the Royal Icing.

2. Divide the Royal Icing and dye each portion with the colors you will use. For each color make stiff icing and loose icing. Put the stiff icing in a pastry bag fitted with the #2 tip and the loose icing in a bag fitted with the #3 tip.

3. Outline and flood the cookies in your desired colors. Let the cookies dry, uncovered, on a flat surface for at least 3 hours.

Techniques for Cookies Pictured

ORANGE BAG: Dye less than 1 ounce (about the size of a marble) of orange fondant for each cookie. On a smooth surface greased with shortening, roll it out to about 1/16 inch thick. For the flap, cut a 1 x 3-inch rectangle and round the edge by cutting away two of the corners. For the corner pieces, cut a circle out of the orange fondant using the 1-inch round cutter. Cut the circle in half and then half again. (You need only two corners for each cookie.)

For the handle, cut a strip of orange fondant approximately 3 inches long and 3/16 inch wide. Use a toothpick to make stitching marks on the handle, flap, and corner pieces. Attach them to the cookie. If they do not stick, use a tiny drop of water to moisten the back of the fondant.

For the clasp, cut a 1/2-inch-long and 1/8-inch-wide strip of orange fondant and curve it before attaching it to the middle of the flap.

STRIPED BAG: Stripes are dyed brown fondant or chocolate fondant attached with a dab of water. The fondant flap is made as above. Pipe dots for the handle and clasp in icing (#1 tip).

PLAID BAG: Outline and flood in icing. Make stripes for plaid in various colors of fondant or gum paste, attach with a dab of water. Use 1 stripe for the handle. Pipe buttons on the handle in stiff icing (#1 tip).

What You Need

COOKIES

1 recipe cookie dough (see *Basic Recipes* pages 53–54)

1 recipe of Royal Icing (page 58)

MATERIALS

Food-coloring gels: rose pink, buckeye brown, sunset orange, leaf green, electric green, navy blue, coal black

4 ounces gum paste or fondant (store-bought or page 60)

Shortening (for rolling out fondant)

EQUIPMENT

4½ x 4¼-inch handbag cookie cutter or template (page 90)

Toothpicks

Pastry bags and plastic couplers

Pastry tips: #1, #2, #3

Scissors

Plastic mat

Small rolling pin

1½-inch round cutter

X-acto knife

Ruler

Stitching tool (optional)

TECHNIQUES

Making a template (page 27)

Dyeing Royal Icing (page 40)

Filling a pastry bag (page 38)

Flooding (page 25)

Dyeing fondant and gum paste (page 40)

Piping dots and straight lines (page 39)

Witch's Wardrobe

YIELD: APPROXIMATELY 12 COOKIES

What You Need

COOKIES

1 recipe cookie dough (see *Basic Recipes* pages 53–54)

1 recipe Royal Icing (page 58)

MATERIALS

Food-coloring gels: coal black, lemon yellow, buckeye brown, sunset orange, leaf green

Black sanding sugar

EQUIPMENT

Boot, hat, and broom cookie cutters or templates (page 91)

Toothpicks

Pastry bags and plastic couplers

Pastry tips: #2, #3

Scissors

TECHNIQUES

Making a template (page 27)

Dyeing Royal Icing (page 40)

Filling a pastry bag (page 38)

Flooding (page 25)

Decorating with sanding sugar (page 27)

Piping dots and straight lines (page 39)

A witch may be spooky, but she has to look stylish, too. Here are a few fashionable cookies for Halloween. We have created all the accessories she needs — boots, brooms, and hats — to complete her closet. Each cookie shape is decorated in a different way. Choose your favorite variation or try them all.

Method

1. Prepare the cookie dough and roll it out as directed. Use the boot, hat, and broom cookie cutters or templates to cut out cookies. Bake as directed in the recipe. Let cookies cool completely. While they are cooling, prepare the Royal Icing.

2. Divide the icing and dye each portion with the colors you will use. For each color make stiff icing and loose icing. Put the stiff icing in a pastry bag fitted with the #2 tip and the loose icing in a bag fitted with a #3 tip.

3. Outline and flood the cookies in your desired colors. Let the cookies dry, uncovered, on a flat surface for at least 3 hours. For an easy version, coat the cookies with sanding sugar before allowing them to dry. Hold the flooded cookie over a bowl and spoon on the sanding sugar. (You need about 3 tablespoons of sanding sugar per cookie.) Let the sanded cookies dry for at least 20 minutes before removing excess sugar.

Techniques for Cookies Pictured

BOOTS: Follow template on page 91 to guide you in making the outline of the three sections for the boot. Striped: Outline and flood in icing. Pipe bow, stripes, and laces in icing (#2 tip). Green: Outline and flood in icing (to create moss green, mix leaf green with a touch of yellow and brown). Pipe laces and stitching in stiff icing (#2 tip).

HATS: Sparkling: Outline and flood in icing. Pipe hat band and bow in icing (#2 tip). Striped: Outline and flood in icing. Pipe hat band and stripes in icing (#2 tip).

BROOMS: Outline and flood in icing. Pipe lines for straw broom head in icing (#3 tip). Each line should start at the bottom of the broom handle and finish at varying lengths to make the broom's bristles. Pipe stitching in icing (#2 tip).

Modern Wedding Vow Cookies

YIELD: APPROXIMATELY 20 TO 24 COOKIES

The cookies are inspired by some beautiful petit fours I once saw at a wedding. I thought it would be a great idea — and much easier — to make them as delicious cookies. The square shape gives them a modern feel. Have fun and make up your own sayings and motifs. I've included a few ideas here to get you started. These cookies also look great with a simple monogram or special date in the center.

Method

1. Prepare the cookie dough and roll it out as directed. Use the square cookie cutter to cut out your cookies. Bake as directed in the recipe. Let cookies cool completely. While they are cooling, prepare the Royal Icing.

2. For the background, make stiff and loose white icing. Put the stiff icing in a pastry bag fitted with the #2 tip and the loose icing in a bag fitted with a #3 tip.

3. Outline and flood the cookies. Let the cookies dry, uncovered, on a flat surface for at least 3 hours.

4. For the overpipe decorations, mix your desired colors of stiff Royal Icing. Follow the instructions for decorating on the next page.

What You Need

COOKIES

1 recipe Vanilla Sugar Cookie dough (page 53)

1 recipe Royal Icing (page 58)

MATERIALS

Food-coloring gels: rose pink, electric pink, lemon yellow, sunset orange, leaf green, electric green, super red, sky blue, buckeye brown

Gold luster dust (optional)

Pure lemon extract

White sanding sugar (optional)

Pink and blue dragées (optional)

EQUIPMENT

2-inch square cookie cutter

Toothpicks

Pastry bags and plastic couplers

Pastry tips: #1, #2, #3

Scissors

1 small paintbrush

TECHNIQUES

Dyeing Royal Icing (page 40)

Filling a pastry bag (page 38)

Flooding (page 25)

Decorating with sanding sugar (page 27)

Piping dots and straight lines (page 39)

Overpiping (page 26)

Techniques for Cookies Pictured

Each design is created using different steps. Below we have outlined the various methods to decorate the cookies pictured here. Pick your favorite vow and make them all the same, make one of each, or come up with your own!

RINGS: Pipe rings in stiff icing (#2 tip), pipe "diamond" in icing (#1) then sprinkle with white sanding sugar. Pipe border dots in icing (#2 tip). Dry for at least 1 hour. Create gold paint with ⅛ teaspoon of gold luster dust and about 1 teaspoon lemon extract and lightly paint the rings.

BIG RED HEART: Pipe border in stiff pink icing (#1 tip). Outline and flood heart in icing. Pipe dots in green icing (#1 tip).

"LOVE": Pipe LOVE in icing (# 2 tip). Pipe border dots in icing (#2 tip). Overpipe border and LOVE in icing (#1 tip).

FLORAL WEDDING CAKE: Pipe cake outline in icing (#1 tip). Pipe flower dots in icing (#1 tip). Pipe border dots in icing (#1 tip).

CHAMPAGNE FLUTES: Pipe flute outlines in stiff icing (#1 tip). Pipe border dots in icing (#1 tip), attach pink dragées immediately. If the icing is drying too quickly, work in sections. Pipe champagne and bubbles in icing (#1 tip). Dry for 1 hour. Create gold paint with ⅛ teaspoon gold luster dust and 1 teaspoon lemon extract. Use a small brush to paint the flutes lightly.

DOTTED WEDDING CAKE: Follow the procedure for the floral wedding cake, piping evenly spaced dots instead of flowers.

"I DO": Pipe I DO in stiff icing (#1 tip). Pipe border in icing (#1 tip) and attach blue dragées immediately. If the icing dries too quickly, work in sections. Overpipe in icing (#1 tip).

"TRUST": Pipe TRUST in stiff icing (#2 tip). Pipe border dots in icing (#1 tip). Overpipe in icing (#1 tip).

PINK AND RED HEART: Outline and flood heart in contrasting colors (#1 tip). Pipe border dots in icing (#1 tip).

Fruit Cookies

YIELD: APPROXIMATELY 12–24 COOKIES, DEPENDING ON HOW YOU SLICE THEM!

What You Need

COOKIES

1 recipe cookie dough (see *Basic Recipes* pages 53–54). Use citrus variation if desired.

1 recipe Royal Icing (page 58)

MATERIALS

Food-coloring gels: rose pink, electric pink, lemon yellow, buckeye brown, sunset orange, leaf green, avocado, super red, coal black

EQUIPMENT

3-inch round cookie cutter or round drinking glass

Ruler

X-acto knife

Toothpicks

Pastry bags and plastic couplers

Pastry tips: #1, #2, #3

Scissors

Small paintbrush with stiff bristles

Small dish of water

TECHNIQUES

Filling a pastry bag (page 38)

Dyeing Royal Icing (page 40)

Flooding (page 25)

Drop-in flooding (page 26)

Piping dots and straight lines (page 39)

Overpiping (page 26)

Brush embroidery (page 43)

These are my favorite cookies to make in the summertime. They are fun and colorful at a pool party or picnic. You don't even need a cutter to make them — just use the top of a round glass.

Method

1.   Prepare the cookie dough and roll it out as directed. Use the round cookie cutter or the top rim of a round glass to cut out cookies. Cut the circles in half for orange and watermelon slices. Bake as directed in the recipe. Let cookies cool. While they are cooling, prepare the Royal Icing.

2.   Divide the icing and dye each portion with the colors desired (see techniques for each cookie for icing consistency). Put the stiff and loose icings in pastry bags fitted with the appropriate tip.

3.   Follow the piping directions on page 87. Let the cookies dry, uncovered, on a flat surface for at least 3 hours.

Techniques for Cookies Pictured

Each design is created using different steps. Below we have outlined the various methods to decorate the cookies pictured here. Pick your favorite fruit and make them all the same, make one of each, or come up with your own!

GRAPEFRUIT HALF: Outline the cookie with stiff lemon yellow icing (#2 tip). With white icing (#2 tip), pipe the rind, then the sections evenly spaced. Pipe one large white dot in the center of the cookie. Use a toothpick to create a half-starburst, pulling the toothpick from the center outward. Fill each section with a small amount of stiff peach icing and use a water-moistened brush to pull the icing and create an uneven look (see brush embroidery, page 43).

ORANGE SLICE: Outline the curved edge of the cookie with stiff dark orange icing (#3 tip). With stiff white icing (#2 tip), pipe the rind straight edge, then sections. Pipe one large dot in the middle of the straight edge of the cookie and use a toothpick to create a half-starburst, pulling the toothpick from the center of the dot outward. For the pulp, fill each section with a small amount of stiff orange icing and use a water-moistened brush to pull the icing and create an uneven look.

WATERMELON SLICE: Outline the curved edge of the cookie with stiff green icing (#2 tip). Pipe stiff white icing (#3 tip) rind. Outline the rest of the cookie with stiff hot pink icing. Let the outline dry for an hour, then flood the cookie with the hot pink. Let it dry for at least 3 hours. Pipe stiff black dots of icing (#1 tip) for the seeds, and immediately pull the dots into the shape of teardrops with the end of a toothpick.

KIWI HALF: Outline the cookie with stiff green icing (#2 tip). For the fuzz, pipe a line of stiff mustard brown icing (#3 tip) outside the green line. Before it dries, use the end of a toothpick to pull the icing out from the cookie. Using loose green icing and loose white icing, drop-in flood a small oval of white icing in the center then quickly flood a ring of green around the white icing, flooding to the green edge. Use a toothpick to pull the white center out toward the green. Let the cookies dry at least 3 hours. Pipe dots of stiff black icing (#1 tip) for the seeds, and immediately pull the dots into the shape of teardrops with the end of a toothpick.

Dragonfly and Butterfly Cookies

YIELD: APPROXIMATELY 12 COOKIES

What You Need

COOKIES

1 recipe cookie dough (see *Basic Recipes* pages 53–54)

1 recipe Royal Icing (page 58)

MATERIALS

4 ounces fondant (store-bought or page 60)

Food-coloring gels: rose pink, lemon yellow, leaf green, buckeye brown, violet

Shortening (for rolling out fondant)

EQUIPMENT

Butterfly cookie cutter or template (page 91)

Dragonfly cookie cutter or template (page 91)

Toothpicks

Pastry bags and plastic couplers

Pastry tips: #2, #3

Scissors

Plastic mat

X-acto knife

Ruler

TECHNIQUES

Making a template (page 27)

Dyeing fondant and gum paste (page 40)

Dyeing Royal Icing (page 40)

Filling a pastry bag (page 38)

Flooding (page 25)

Drop-in flooding (page 26)

These cookies remind me of springtime. We have made them for birthday parties, wedding favors, and bridal and baby showers. They are perfect for Mother's Day, Easter, or any occasion that calls for something pretty.

Method

1. Prepare the cookie dough and roll it out as directed. Use butterfly and dragonfly cookie cutters or templates to cut out cookies. Bake as directed in the recipe. Let cookies cool completely. While they are cooling, prepare the Royal Icing.

2. Divide the fondant in half and dye the colors of fondant for the bodies of the butterflies and dragonflies: pale green for the dragonflies and brown for the butterflies. (If you have chocolate fondant, use it for the butterflies.) Form the bodies using a dab of shortening and mold the fondant in your hands. **For the butterflies,** roll a ball for the head approximately ⅜ inch in diameter. To make the body, form a cone approximately ¼ inch wide and 1½ inches long then pinch the end to sculpt the tail into a sharp point.

For the dragonflies, roll a ball and pinch it between your fingers to form a head approximately ½ inch wide by ¼ inch long. Make two sections for the body. The mid-section is ⅜ inch wide by ⅝ inch long. The tail is ¼ inch wide and 2 inches long. Sculpt these sections by rolling the fondant into a log, cutting at the appropriate length, and shaping the ends (the tail should come gradually to a point) with your hands. Attach the sections to the cookies using a dab of icing or water.

3. Prepare stiff and loose icing in pale violet and yellow, plus pale pink loose icing (for drop-in flooding). Put the stiff icings in pastry bags fitted with the #2 tip and the flood icings in bags fitted with a #3 tip.

4. Outline and flood the **butterfly wings,** one wing at a time, in violet. Before the wing dries, on the upper wings drop-in flood six dots of the pale pink icing. On the bottom wings, drop-in flood three dots then pull gently from the center with a toothpick to create teardrop shapes.

5. Outline and flood the **dragonfly wings,** one wing at a time, in yellow. Before the icing dries, drop-in flood one large pale pink dot and pull gently from the center with a toothpick to create a teardrop shape.

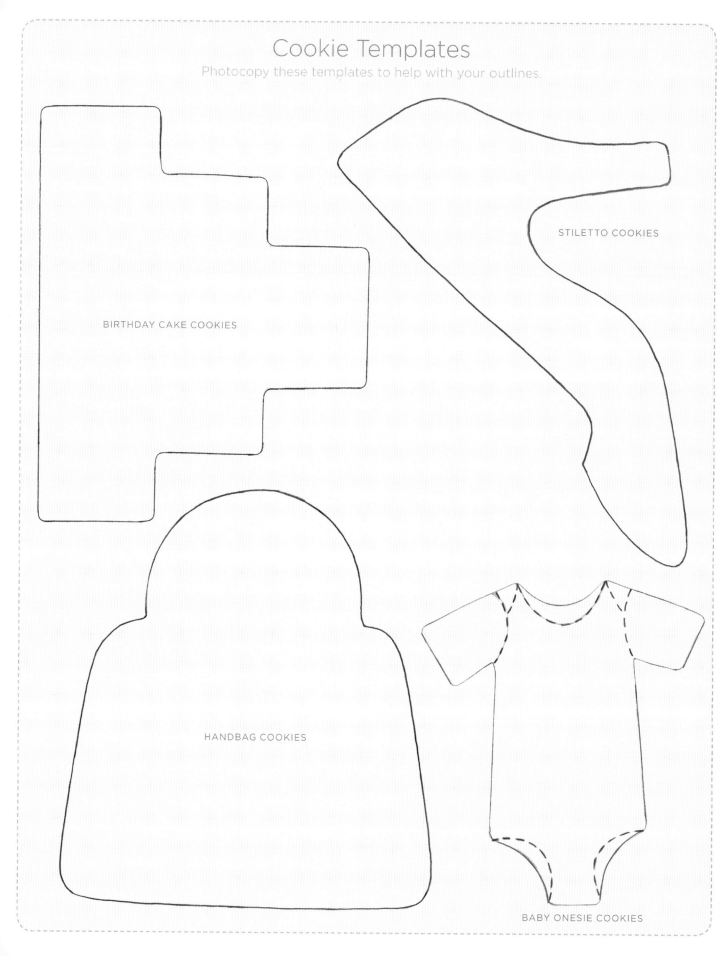

Cookie Templates

Photocopy these templates to help with your outlines.

STILETTO COOKIES

BIRTHDAY CAKE COOKIES

HANDBAG COOKIES

BABY ONESIE COOKIES

Cookie Templates

Photocopy these templates to help with your outlines.

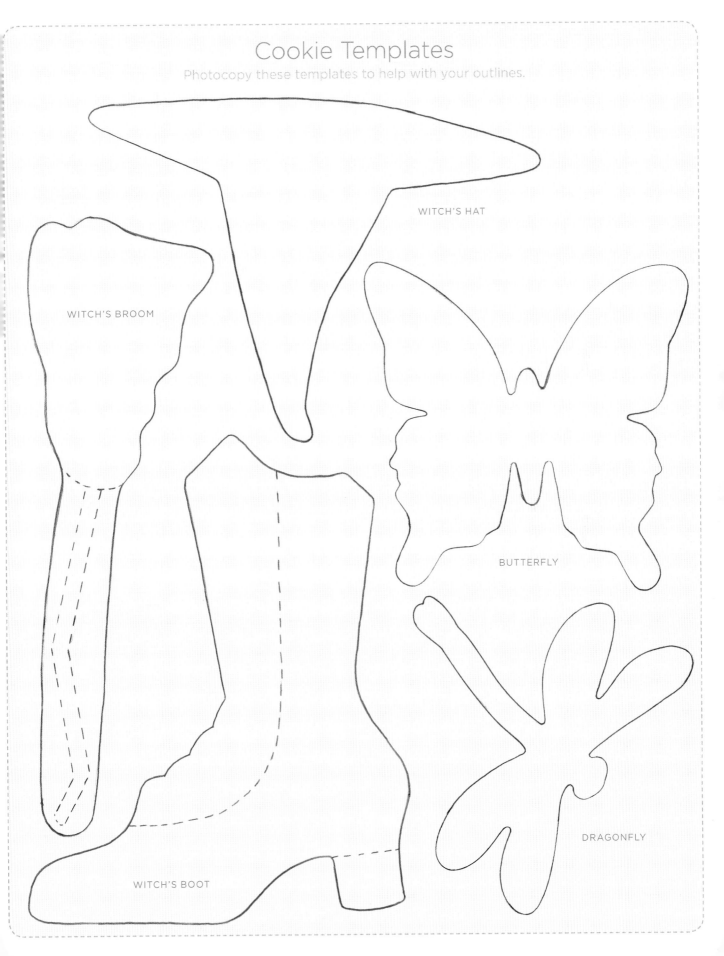

WITCH'S HAT

WITCH'S BROOM

BUTTERFLY

DRAGONFLY

WITCH'S BOOT

Cupcakes

Everyone loves cupcakes. They are often the most coveted of desserts at parties, showers, and weddings. Each guest gets her very own little sweet to devour. Cupcakes have come a long way in the last few years, and they have become a hot trend for birthday parties and weddings.

Cupcakes are created from three edible elements: delicious cake, yummy frosting, and the adorable decoration. To make a fabulous cupcake, use our recipes for the cake and frosting (see *Basic Recipes* pages 48–52 for cakes and page 55 for frosting). To save time, you can make cupcakes from a mix and use store-bought frosting. It might not taste quite the same as if you made it from scratch, but we know you're busy. If you decide to do that, work with the best quality mix and frosting you can find.

Our Swiss-Meringue Buttercream (page 56) is smooth, thick, and less sweet than our cupcake frosting, and is great for making swirls. If you do not need to make a swirl, you can use the cupcake frosting or ganache.

For the decoration, go wild — this is the fun part! There are two key things to consider: the decoration on top of the cupcake, of course, and also the wrapper. If you are making a winter-themed cupcake, for example, choose a silver wrapper. If you are showing off some beautiful sugar flowers, consider a chocolate brown wrapper that resembles dirt but is still a chic shade. Or check out the newest designs in wrappers, which range from stripes and polka dots to metallic colors and character motifs perfect for a child's birthday. When you are choosing the flavor of your cake, always think about the color wrapper you want to use. If you are baking a dark cake like chocolate, do not use a pastel cupcake wrapper unless you want the cake color to show through. Pastel cake wrappers look much better with vanilla or light-colored cake; chocolate cake is best with solid dark-colored or metallic wrappers.

HOT TIPS

■ To make cupcakes look extra special for a baby or bridal shower, wrap a ribbon or tie a bow around the edge of each wrapper.

■ Instead of just serving cupcakes on a tray, find a plastic tier or tiered plates for a pretty presentation. Displaying cupcakes on tiers can elevate the importance of these little desserts.

■ To make your cupcakes unforgettable: add a filling! Before the layer of frosting, add a layer of preserves, a little squirt of Chocolate Ganache (page 57), or a layer of Simple Syrup (page 59) to add a hint of flavor.

Crystal Cupcakes

YIELD: 24 CUPCAKES

What You Need

CUPCAKES

1 cake recipe, any flavor
(see *Basic Recipes* pages 49–52)

1 frosting recipe (see *Basic Recipes* pages 55–57)

MATERIALS

1½ cups (12 ounces) vodka

Food-coloring gels: bakers rose, super red

2 pounds rock candy crystals

EQUIPMENT

Trays lined with parchment or wax paper

Metal bowl

Toothpicks

Strainer

Cupcake tins

Pale pink cupcake wrappers

Small offset spatula

TECHNIQUES

Creating a dome of filling (page 28)

About four years ago I worked on a book with Swarovski, the world-famous crystal manufacturer. For the book I created cupcakes and cakes that featured their beautiful crystals. The pieces were magnificent, but there was one problem: they were inedible. Clients constantly ask for "crystals" on their cakes, so finally I created my own version of beautiful crystals that you can eat by dyeing ordinary rock candy with stunning colors to make it look like shimmering crystal.

Method

AT LEAST 1 DAY IN ADVANCE: DYE THE ROCK CANDY CRYSTALS

1. Combine the vodka and ¼ teaspoon of pink or red food coloring in a metal bowl. Stir to distribute the food coloring evenly.

2. Place a handful of rock candy crystals in a strainer and lower the strainer into the vodka mixture. After a few seconds remove the strainer from the bowl, allowing the excess liquid to drain back into the bowl. If the color is too dark, add some more vodka or water to lighten it.

3. Spread the dyed rock candy crystals in a single layer on a tray lined with parchment paper and let them dry overnight.

4. Repeat this procedure with the rest of your rock candy crystals. If you want more than one color (at least three shades will provide a nice assortment), start with the lightest shade, then add more food coloring to the vodka to adjust the color of the rock candy crystals and color the next set. The longer you keep the strainer in the mixture the darker the crystals will become. Keep the different colors separate while drying.

MAKE AND ASSEMBLE THE CUPCAKES

1. Prepare the cake batter as directed. Line the cupcake tins with wrappers. Fill each halfway with batter and bake the cupcakes as directed by the recipe. Let them cool completely.

2. While cupcakes are cooling, make the frosting.

3. When they are cool, frost the cupcakes with a dome of frosting.

4. Use a spoon or your hands to pile the colored rock candy crystals onto the cupcakes. If the candy is not sticking to itself to create the height you want, spritz it with some water. Let the cupcakes set for 10 to 15 minutes.

Polka-Dot Cupcakes

YIELD: 24 CUPCAKES

This design couldn't be sweeter or easier to accomplish. These cupcakes make a statement without a lot of work. In pastel colors they are perfect for a baby or bridal shower. For a fun fiesta, use bright, bold colors. Polka dots like this are fabulous on any cupcake, cake, or cookie. If you do not like fondant, arrange the polka dots on smooth buttercream.

Method

1. Prepare the cake batter as directed. Line the cupcake tins with wrappers. Fill each halfway with batter and bake the cupcakes as directed by the recipe. Let them cool completely.

2. While cupcakes are cooking, prepare the frosting.

3. Divide the rolled fondant into three equal portions and dye the portions light pink, light blue, and light green. Work with one color at a time and wrap the other two in plastic wrap until ready to use.

4. Frost the cupcakes with a dome of filling. On a surface greased with shortening, roll out the fondant to ⅛ inch thick. Work with one color at a time. Use the round cookie cutter to cut circles of fondant. Smooth the circles onto the cupcakes.

5. Once all the cupcakes are covered with fondant, make the polka dots. Roll out the desired color of fondant on the greased surface to approximately ¹⁄₁₆ inch thick. You will need about 16 dots per cupcake. Use the #10 tip to cut out the polka dots. Using a brush dampened with water, attach the polka dots to the surface of the cupcake.

6. **OPTIONAL:** Make bows out of ribbon and attach the ribbon with hot glue to the cupcake wrapper, about ⅔ of the way up from the bottom of the cupcake.

HOT TIPS

▪ You can easily turn these dots into buttons by poking two holes in them with a toothpick. Or use small cutters to create hearts and stars instead of dots. The options are endless.

▪ For holiday cupcakes, use gold wrappers, green fondant, and red polka dots. For chic French cupcakes, use chocolate brown wrappers, pink fondant, and chocolate brown dots. For a fiesta, use yellow wrappers, hot pink fondant, and orange polka dots. For Halloween, use black wrappers with orange fondant and black dots.

What You Need

CUPCAKES

1 cake recipe, any flavor
(see *Basic Recipes* pages 49–52)

1 frosting recipe (pages 55–57)

MATERIALS

2 pounds fondant (store-bought or page 60)

Shortening (for rolling out fondant)

Food-coloring gels: bakers rose, willow green, royal blue

EQUIPMENT

Cupcake tins

Pastel cupcake wrappers (pink, blue, and yellow)

Toothpicks

Small offset spatula

Plastic mat

Small rolling pin

2½-inch round cookie cutter

#10 pastry tip

Small paintbrush

Small dish of water

Ribbon (optional)

Glue gun (optional)

TECHNIQUES

Dyeing fondant and gum paste (page 40)

Creating a dome of filling (page 28)

Covering cupcakes in fondant (page 29)

Sports Cupcakes

YIELD: 24 CUPCAKES

What You Need

CUPCAKES

1 cake recipe, any flavor
 (see *Basic Recipes* pages 49–52)

1 frosting recipe (see *Basic Recipes* pages 55–57)

½ recipe Royal Icing (page 58)

MATERIALS

2 pounds fondant (store-bought or page 60)

Shortening (for rolling out fondant)

Food-coloring gels: lemon yellow, sunset orange, coal black

EQUIPMENT

Cupcake tins

Red cupcake wrappers

Toothpicks

Small offset spatula

Plastic mat

Small rolling pin

2½-inch round cookie cutter

Gum-paste veining tool or scalpel

Pastry tips: #2, #3

Pastry bag and coupler

Red food marker

TECHNIQUES

Dyeing fondant and gum paste (page 40)

Creating a dome of filling (page 28)

Covering cupcakes in fondant (page 29)

Dyeing Royal Icing (page 40)

My family is filled with sports fanatics, so I just love making these cupcakes to celebrate birthdays and sporting events. They are the perfect dessert to accompany a barbeque or an afternoon watching the playoffs.

Method

1. Prepare the cake batter as directed. Line the cupcake tins with wrappers. Fill each halfway with batter and bake the cupcakes as directed by the recipe. Let them cool completely.

2. While the cupcakes are cooling, make the frosting.

3. Divide the fondant into three equal portions. Keep one portion white and dye the other two orange and yellow. Work with one color and wrap the other two in plastic wrap until ready to use.

4. Frost the cupcakes with a dome of filling. On a surface greased with shortening, roll out the fondant to approximately ⅛ inch thick, working with one color at a time. Use the round cookie cutter to cut out circles of fondant.

5. Since the fondant dries quickly you will want to create the decorations for each cupcake as you cover it. Follow the directions for the particular sports cupcake you are making.

Basketball

1. Cover the cupcake with orange fondant.

2. Use the back of a scalpel or veining tool to make the four lines found on a basketball. The lines need to be ⅛ inch deep so you can fill them in with Royal Icing later.

3. Gently press a #3 tip into the fondant to create the texture of a basketball, staying within the lines of each section.

4. Dye half the Royal Icing black and put it in a pastry bag fitted with a #2 tip. Carefully squeeze the icing into the lines you created.

Tennis Ball

1. Cover the cupcake with yellow fondant.

2. Use the back of a scalpel or veining tool to make the seams of a tennis ball. The lines need to be ⅛ inch deep so you can fill them in with Royal Icing later.

3. Fill a pastry bag fitted with a #2 tip with white Royal Icing. Carefully squeeze the icing into the lines you created.

Baseball

1. Cover the cupcake with white fondant.

2. Using a toothpick, outline the seams of the baseball. Using a red food marker, draw the stitching lines of a baseball on the white fondant. To practice, draw a circle on a piece of paper and create the lines before trying them on the cupcake. If you make a mistake, use a little water or vodka (don't worry — it evaporates) and a cotton swab to take the marker away. Let it dry and start again.

Pool Ball Cupcakes

YIELD: 24 CUPCAKES

One of my favorite sculpted cakes was a pool table with pool balls. The bride surprised the groom with a cake representing one of his favorite pastimes. Since each ball is a different color, pool balls also make great cupcakes. Make these for a pool party in the summer (get it?) or for a game-night party. Use green felt to create a pool table.

What You Need

CUPCAKES

1 cake recipe, any flavor (see *Basic Recipes* pages 49–52)

1 frosting recipe (see *Basic Recipes* pages 55–57)

MATERIALS

3 pounds fondant (store-bought or page 60)

Shortening (for rolling out fondant)

Food-coloring gels: lemon yellow, sunset orange, leaf green, royal blue, violet, maroon, super red, coal black

EQUIPMENT

Cupcake tins

Chocolate brown cupcake wrappers

Small offset spatula

Plastic mat

Small rolling pin

Round cookie cutters (1 inch, 2½ inches, 3½ inches)

Toothpicks

Ruler

Paring knife or X-acto knife

Black food marker

TECHNIQUES

Creating a dome of filling (page 28)

Covering cupcakes in fondant (page 29)

Dyeing fondant and gum paste (page 40)

Method

1. Prepare the cake batter as directed. Line the cupcake tins with wrappers. Fill each halfway with batter and bake the cupcakes as directed by the recipe. Let them cool completely.

2. While the cupcakes are cooling, make the frosting.

3. Frost the cupcakes with a dome of filling.

4. On a surface greased with shortening, roll out 1 pound undyed fondant to ⅛ inch thick. Use the 2½-inch round cookie cutter to cut out circles of fondant. Smooth the fondant onto the cupcake. Cover at least 16 cupcakes and set aside one cupcake for the cue ball.

5. Divide the remaining fondant into 2-ounce pieces. Dye each piece with the following ball colors: yellow, orange, green, blue, purple, maroon, red, and black. You will create one solid ball and one striped ball with each of these colors except for the black, which you'll use only for the solid 8 ball.

6. On the greased surface, roll out one color at a time to approximately ¹⁄₁₆ inch thick and create the solid and striped ball for that color at the same time. This will cut down on the time it takes you to roll out each color.

SOLID: Use the 3½-inch round cutter to cut out a circle of fondant. Use the 1-inch cutter to cut out a circle in the center of the fondant piece; this is where the ball's number will show.

Cut out some of the holes off-center but don't get too close to the edge. Different cutouts will make the balls look like they are moving. Smooth the piece of fondant over the white fondant on each cupcake. If it is not sticking, moisten it with a drop of water.

STRIPED: Using a knife and ruler, cut out a strip of fondant, 3½ inches long by 1¾ inch wide, from the rolled-out color. Use the 1-inch round cutter to cut out the hole where the number will show. Smooth the piece of fondant onto the cupcake. If it is not sticking, moisten the round with a drop of water. You may need to trim the edges of the stripe once you place the colored fondant on the cupcake. The only color not to get a stripe is black.

7. Once all of the cupcakes are covered, use the black food marker to write the number on the ball. The following chart will help you put the right number on the right color.

COLOR	# FOR SOLID	# FOR STRIPE
Black	8	none
Green	6	14
Red	3	11
Maroon	7	15
Purple	4	12
Yellow	1	9
Orange	5	13
Blue	2	10

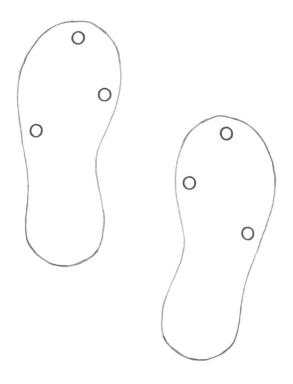

What You Need

CUPCAKES

1 cake recipe, any flavor
(see *Basic Recipes* pages 49–52)

1 frosting recipe (see *Basic Recipes*
pages 55–57)

MATERIALS

1½ pounds fondant (store-bought
 or page 60) or gum paste

Shortening (for rolling out fondant
or gum paste)

Food-coloring gels: electric pink,
electric green, fucshia

3 cups brown sugar

EQUIPMENT

Toothpicks

Plastic mat

Small rolling pin

Paring knife or X-acto knife

Small 5-petal flower cutter

Paper towels

Cupcake tins

Yellow cupcake wrappers

Small offset spatula

Small paintbrush

Small dish of water

TECHNIQUES

Dyeing fondant and gum paste
(page 40)

Creating a dome of filling
(page 28)

Flip-Flop Cupcakes

YIELD: 24 CUPCAKES

These flip-flops remind me of my friend Ashley. She is always wearing them on her way to the beach, out to shop, or after one of her long runs. These cupcakes are fun for any beach or pool party or anytime you want to celebrate the summer!

Method

1. Dye all the colors of fondant or gum paste. For each cupcake you will need approximately 1 ounce of fondant. Dye half fondant electric pink and divide the remaining fondant. Tint half electric green for the straps and half fuchsia for the flowers.

2. On a plastic mat greased with shortening, roll out the electric pink fondant or gum paste to approximately ⅛ inch thick. Using your X-acto knife, cut out the shape of the two flip-flops. Photocopy or trace the template (page 105). Use your fingers, coated with shortening, to smooth the edges.

3. To form the straps, roll out the electric green fondant or gum paste into a thin cord, less than 1⁄16 inch wide. Cut one 1-inch-long piece and one ½-inch-long piece per flip-flop. Use a toothpick to create three holes in each flip-flop. Moisten the ends of the straps and insert the ends into the holes, bringing the straps together to meet at the front hole. Insert a small piece of rolled paper towel under the straps to hold them up.

4. Roll out the fuchsia fondant or gum paste to approximately 1⁄16 inch thick on a plastic mat greased with shortening. Cut out the 5-petal flowers, moisten the back with a dab of water, and stick it to the straps of the flip-flops. Roll a tiny ball of green, moisten it, and stick in the center of the flower. Let them dry overnight on crumpled paper towels to keep their shape.

MAKE AND ASSEMBLE THE CUPCAKES

1. Prepare the cake batter as directed. Line the cupcake tins with wrappers. Fill each halfway with batter and bake the cupcakes as directed by the recipe. Let them cool completely.

2. While the cupcakes are cooling, make the frosting.

3. Frost the cupcakes with a dome of filling. Dunk the frosted cupcakes into a bowl of brown sugar to create the "sand."

4. Remove the toweling from the straps of the flip-flops and place them on the cupcakes. If they do not stick right away, use an extra dab of filling to hold them.

HOT TIP

■ Replace the brown sugar "sand" with some green buttercream grass (use the piping tip called a "grass tip," or ATECO Tip #133 or Wilton #233) to get a completely different look.

Seashell Cupcakes

I have loved to collect seashells ever since I was a little girl. My mom and I would comb the beach to find the perfect pieces to add to our collection. I love creating these cupcakes for bridal showers or weddings with a beach theme. They are elegant yet fun at the same time. The decorations we make here are made entirely by hand but there are molds of seashells available from specialty cake-decorating stores.

What You Need

CUPCAKES

1 cake recipe, any flavor
(see *Basic Recipes* pages 49–52)

1 Swiss-Meringue Buttercream recipe,
tinted pale blue (page 56)

MATERIALS

1 to 2 pounds gum paste or fondant, depending on the types of shells (see Method
for amounts)

Shortening (for rolling out gum paste)

Food-coloring gels: royal blue,
buckeye brown

Food-coloring powder: brown

EQUIPMENT

Plastic mat

Small rolling pin

2¼-inch round cookie cutter

Pastry tips: #4, #10, #806

Toothpicks

Paper towels

Cupcake tins

Paring knife or X-acto knife

Pale blue cupcake wrappers

Pastry bag

Small paintbrush

TECHNIQUES

Dyeing fondant and gum paste
(page 40)

Filling a pastry bag (page 38)

Creating a swirl of frosting
(page 28)

Measuring Gum Paste and Fondant
(page 61)

Method

TWO DAYS IN ADVANCE: MAKE THE SHELLS

Sand Dollars

1.   Approximately 1 ounce of gum paste makes 6 sand dollars. On a plastic mat greased with shortening, roll out white gum paste to ¹⁄₁₆ inch thick. Use a 2¼-inch round cookie cutter and cut out a circle. Peel away the excess gum paste, wrap it in plastic wrap, and save it for later.

2.   Use the top of a #10 tip to cut away two half circles on the bottom edge of the sand dollar. Use the top of a #4 tip to make one larger slit between the two half circles, and 5 smaller slits around the sand dollar.

3.   Use a toothpick to create the design in the center of a sand dollar. Let them dry on a tray of rumpled paper toweling with a slight bend in the middle to give them a curved shape.

Starfish

1.   Approximately 6 ounces of gum paste makes 6 starfish. Dye the gum paste brown. On a plastic mat greased with shortening, roll 1 ounce into a ball and pat it into a round disc. Use the rolling pin and, starting in the center, roll the edges of the disc until they are slightly thinner than the center of the disc, similar to a Frisbee. Using a paring knife, cut out the rough shape of a star (don't worry if the sections are not even).

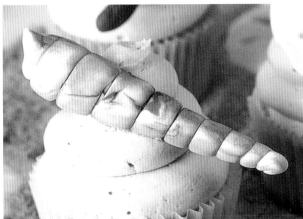

2.   Using a smudge of shortening on your fingers, carefully round the edges of each point and smooth the edges to make the general shape of a starfish. Use the top of a #4 pastry tip and emboss circles all over the starfish, giving it texture. Do not cut through the starfish.

3.   Let the starfish dry with a slight bend in the middle on a tray of rumpled paper toweling. Once dry, dust the starfish with the brown food-coloring powder to add more texture.

Shells

1.   Approximately 2 ounces of gum paste makes 6 shells. Twist ½ ounce of brown gum paste into the remaining white gum paste (refer to steps 1–3 of the wood-staining technique, page 42) until marbleized.

2.   Divide the marbleized gum paste into 6 pieces and roll each piece into a long cone, approximately 2½ inches long. Use a knife to make about 8 slits, on a diagonal, at even intervals along the cone. Make sure the knife goes all the way around the circumference of the cone in order to keep the shape round and the slits look like they run continuously around the body of the shell.

3.   Use your hands to mold the shell into its proper shape before it dries. Pinch the wider end to give it a small point and round the smaller end. Let the shell dry on a flat surface. Once dry, dust it with the brown food-coloring powder to add more texture.

MAKE AND ASSEMBLE THE CUPCAKES

1.   Prepare the cake batter as directed. Line the cupcake tins with wrappers. Fill each halfway with batter and bake the cupcakes as directed by the recipe. Let them cool completely.

2.   While cupcakes are cooling, make the frosting.

3.   Fill a pastry bag fitted with a #806 pastry tip. Since this is a larger tip you do not need the plastic coupler. Frost the cupcakes with a swirl of frosting.

4.   Once the cupcakes are frosted, place them in the refrigerator for about an hour. This allows the frosting to set and makes it easier to place the sugar decorations on top. Gently press the decorations into the buttercream until they feel secure.

HOT TIP

■ If you are serving all the cupcakes together, sprinkle brown sugar on a cake stand or on the table to create a beach scene.

Snowman Cupcakes

YIELD: 24 CUPCAKES

Make these in your warm house while it's snowy and cold outside or bring them to a holiday party. **These little guys make any occasion festive.**

Method

ONE DAY IN ADVANCE: MAKE THE DECORATIONS

1. Use approximately 1 ounce of fondant to make three balls for each snowman. The balls should be 1 inch, ¾ inch, and ½ inch in diameter. Spritz the balls with water and roll them in sanding sugar. Allow them to dry overnight.

MAKE AND ASSEMBLE THE CUPCAKES

1. Prepare the cake batter as directed. Line the cupcake tins with wrappers. Fill each halfway with batter and bake the cupcakes as directed by the recipe. Let them cool completely.

2. While cupcakes are cooling, make the frosting.

3. Frost the cupcakes with a dome of frosting. Dunk the frosted cupcakes into a bowl of white sanding sugar.

4. Hold the toothpick in one hand and, starting with the largest, slide all three "snowballs" onto the toothpick, leaving some room at the bottom to stick into the cupcake. It's okay if some toothpick shows through the top — it will be covered by the hat. Stick the snowman into the center of the cupcake.

5. Color the remaining fondant or gum paste orange, black, red, and green. You need approximately ¼ ounce of orange and black per snowman and 1 ounce of green and red per snowman.

6. To make the hat, roll out a ball of fondant or gum paste and form it into a cone, approximately ½ inch wide at the base and ½ inch tall. Using a contrasting color, roll out a ¼-inch ball for the pom-pom. Stick the pom-pom on the top of the hat with a dab of water. Next roll out a thin strip of the same color, approximately ⅛ inch wide and 2½ inches long. Moisten it with water and place it along the edge of the hat to form the brim. Attach the hat to the top of the snowman's head with a dab of water.

7. To make the scarf, roll out a small piece of fondant or gum paste, approximately 6 inches long and ¼ inch wide. Using a paring knife or scalpel, cut a few slits on each end to create the fringe on the scarf. Gently pick up the scarf and wrap it around the neck of the snowman. Apply a dab of water to stick the scarf together where it meets.

8. For the carrot nose, form a cone ¼ inch long out of the orange fondant or gum paste and attach it in the center of the snowman's face with a tiny dab of water.

9. Roll out the black fondant to approximately ⅛ inch thick. Use the point of a #4 tip to cut out 5 circles, 2 for the eyes and 3 for buttons. Attach them to the snowman with tiny dabs of water.

HOT TIP

■ If you are serving all the cupcakes together, use some extra white sanding sugar or granulated sugar to create a snow scene.

Rubber Duckie Cupcakes

YIELD: 24 CUPCAKES

One of my favorite things to do is replicate a toy in sugar. It is fun to trick people and see if they can tell what is real or not . . . or in this case edible! These little duckies are a favorite toy and are the perfect topping on cupcakes for baby showers or a child's birthday.

Method

ONE DAY IN ADVANCE: MAKE THE DUCKIES

1. Dye approximately 2 ounces of gum paste yellow (I recommend gum paste but if you only have fondant that is fine). Coat your hands with shortening and mold the head by rolling a ball approximately 1 inch in diameter. Form the body with double the amount of gum paste that you used for the head. The body should be pointy on the tail side and rounded to form the chest of the duckie. You may need to cut one side to make the point for the tail. Attach the head to the body with a dab of water.

2. To make the wings, roll out the remaining yellow gum paste to ⅛ inch on a smooth surface greased with shortening. Cut out all of the wings with a paring knife or X-acto knife and attach them to the sides of the duckies' bodies with a dab of water.

3. Dye approximately ¼ ounce of gum paste orange for each beak. Form small cones and use the knife to create an indent to divide the cones in half from the pointy end, but do not cut all the way through. Use a toothpick or a pastry tip to create a small opening for the beaks. Attach the beaks with a dab of water to the duckies' faces.

What You Need

CUPCAKES

1 cake recipe, any flavor
(see *Basic Recipes* pages 49–52)

1 frosting recipe
(see *Basic Recipes* pages 55–57)

MATERIALS

4 pounds of gum paste
(2½ ounces per duckie)

1 pound, 10 ounces fondant
(store-bought or page 60)

Food-coloring gels: sky blue, lemon yellow, sunset orange, coal black

Shortening (for rolling out fondant and gum paste)

EQUIPMENT

Toothpicks

Plastic mat

Small rolling pin

Paring knife or X-acto knife

Small paintbrush

Dish of water

Pastry tips: #4, #7, #10

2½-inch round cookie cutter

Cupcake tins

White brioche molds or cupcake wrappers

Small offset spatula

TECHNIQUES

Dyeing fondant and gum paste (page 40)

Creating a dome of filling (page 28)

Covering cupcakes in fondant (page 29)

Measuring gum paste and fondant (page 61)

4. For each set of eyes, dye a pea-size amount of gum paste black and roll it out to ¹⁄₁₆ inch thick on a smooth surface greased with shortening. Roll out a pea-size piece of white gum paste. Use piping tips #10 and #4 to cut out white circles, you will need two of each size. Mold the larger of the two circles into a slightly oval shape. Use a #7 tip to cut out two black circles. Attach the black circles to the oval white circles with a tiny dab of water. Place the black circle against the top edge of one of the ovals. Attach the smallest white circle on top of the black. Attach them with tiny dabs of water. You should place the eyes so you can see them from both the front and sides of the duckie.

MAKE AND ASSEMBLE THE CUPCAKES

1. Prepare the cake batter as directed. Line the cupcake tins with the brioche molds or cupcake wrappers. Fill each halfway full and bake the cupcakes as directed in the recipe. Let them cool completely.

2. While the cupcakes are cooling, make the frosting.

3. Tint the fondant sky blue, reserving 2 ounces white fondant to make the polka dots.

4. Frost the cupcakes with a dome of cupcake frosting. On a surface greased with shortening, roll out the blue fondant to approximately ⅛ inch thick. If you are using brioche molds, first cut out a circle then use the top edge of an empty mold as a cutter to cut out the fluted design. If you are using standard cupcake wrappers, use a round cutter and cut out a circle of fondant. Smooth the piece of fondant onto the dome of frosting.

5. Place the duckies into the centers of the cupcakes using a toothpick or water. (If they do not stick with water and you do not want to use toothpicks you can use Royal Icing.)

6. Roll out the remaining 2 ounces of white fondant to approximately ¹⁄₁₆ inch thick on the greased surface. Use the #10 tip and cut out 8 to 10 polka dots for each cupcake. Attach them to the blue fondant, around the duckie, with tiny dabs of water.

Hydrangea Cupcakes

YIELD: 24 CUPCAKES

These are beautiful cupcakes that will make your guests ooh and aah when you tell them they are not real flowers. They are popular during the springtime for celebrating weddings and all festive occasions.

Method

TWO DAYS IN ADVANCE: MAKE THE FLOWERS AND LEAVES

The number of flowers you use on each cupcake is up to you. You need 5 to 7 flowers for an average cupcake. If you are making a large number of cupcakes, 3 flowers may work just as well, and if you want very full bouquets you can add more than 7.

1. To make the flowers, dye 1 to 2 pounds of the gum paste lilac (depending on how many flowers you want to make).

2. Create hooks on the end of the wire pieces.

3. See the illustrations on page 118 for these step-by-step instructions. (A) Form a ½-inch ball of lilac gum paste and use the side of the ball tool to create edges. There should be a point in the center and the sides should be thinned, similar to a sombrero. (B) Center the flower cutter over the middle and cut out the hydrangea. (C) Turn the flower over and use the large end of the ball tool to thin the petals. (D) Use the small end of the ball tool to make a small indent in the center of the flower. (E) Moisten the hook end of the wire with a tiny dab of egg white. Pass the wire through the center of the flower. The small hook should catch directly in the center. Mold each petal to give it its own shape and pinch the back of the flower to the wire. (F) Let the flower dry upside down for 2 days. The wire can hook onto a cooling rack placed on a bowl.

What You Need

CUPCAKES

1 cake recipe, any flavor
(see *Basic Recipes* pages 49–52)

1 Chocolate Ganache (page 57) or Chocolate Buttercream recipe (page 56)

½ recipe Royal Icing (page 58)

4 cups (about 1 pound) chocolate wafer cookies, crumbled for "dirt"

MATERIALS

2 to 3 pounds gum paste (the amount you need depends on the number of flowers desired)

Food-coloring gels: violet, willow green

Powdered food coloring: violet, red, green

Shortening (for rolling out gum paste)

¼ cup pasteurized egg whites

EQUIPMENT

Toothpicks

#22-gauge green cloth-covered wires, cut into 4-inch pieces

Ball tool

Hydrangea flower cutter (see Hot Tips)

2 paintbrushes

Plastic mat

Small rolling pin

Leaf cutter

Leaf-veining mold

Paring knife or X-acto knife

Egg carton

Cupcake tins

Chocolate brown cupcake wrappers

Small offset spatula

Pastry bag and coupler

#2 pastry tip

Scissors

TECHNIQUES

Dyeing fondant and gum paste (page 40)

Creating a dome of filling (page 28)

Measuring gum paste and fondant (page 61)

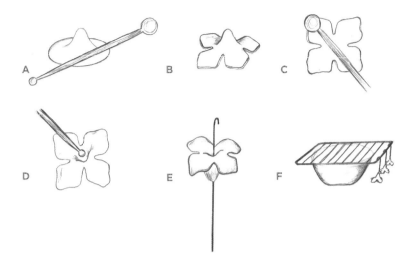

4. Once the flowers have hardened, dust the edges with violet and red food powder and a dry brush. Use a drop of white Royal Icing or a small ball of gum paste to create the center of the flower.

5. To make the leaves, color approximately 1 pound of gum paste leaf green. On a plastic mat greased with shortening, roll out to ⅛ inch thick. Using the leaf cutter or a paring knife, cut out at least 1 leaf per cupcake.

6. Moisten one end of a cloth-covered wire with a tiny dab of egg white. Hold the leaf between your thumb and index finger, and carefully pass the wire from the bottom of the leaf halfway into the gum paste. If the leaf starts to tear, try rolling the gum paste thicker.

7. Once the wire is inserted into the leaf, press the leaf into the veining mold. Place the leaves in an egg carton and let dry overnight. Once they have hardened, dust the edges with green food powder and a dry brush.

MAKE AND ASSEMBLE THE CUP-CAKES

1. Prepare the cake batter as directed. Line the cupcake tins with wrappers. Fill each halfway with batter and bake the cupcakes as directed by the recipe. Let them cool completely.

2. While cupcakes are cooling, make the frosting.

3. Frost the cupcakes with a dome of chocolate frosting. Dunk the frosted cupcakes into a bowl of chocolate cake crumbs (see Hot Tips).

4. Take a few flowers at a time and twist their wires together to form a bunch. Either cut the excess wire or fold the wire up and place the bunch in the center of the cupcake. Take one or two leaves and insert them into the cupcake as you like.

HOT TIPS

▪ If you are short on time, you can buy both the leaves and the flowers already made from cake-decorating stores. Just dust them with some powdered food coloring to create the colors you like.

▪ If you do not have a hydrangea flower cutter, form a small cone of violet gum paste and use a pair of scissors to cut 4 slits into the fatter end of the cone. Using your fingers, flatten each section into 4 flower petals. Insert the wire as instructed above.

▪ These flowers would look great in the plastic pot of the Tomato Mini Cake (page 124). And the tomato (a slightly smaller size) would look cute on top of these cupcakes.

Mini Cakes

Mini Cakes

Mini cakes are small creations that serve one to two people. Unlike cupcakes, which all have the same shape and form to start, these are individually sculpted and decorated in a range of designs. Mini cakes can be beautiful, but they can also take quite a bit of effort. In fact, in some cases they require *more* time and effort than large cakes because each individual cake has so much detail — which means repeating your efforts and multiplying the time requirements. We do not recommend making complicated mini cakes for each guest at a party for 100 people. When you do make them, though, people will adore them. Individual mini cakes are stunning gifts, and a small group of mini cakes grouped together makes a striking impression.

Most of the cakes in this chapter are fondant covered, except for the party hats, which are decorated with dots of buttercream. Mastering the art of covering a cake with fondant means you can tackle any project in this chapter or the Cakes chapter — it is a great skill to have and it is the secret to making cakes that look like real-life objects. For most of the projects in this chapter, you can use any cake and filling recipe you wish. For cakes that require sculpting, I always recommend a sturdy filling such as our Swiss-Meringue Buttercream (page 56) or Ganache (page 57).

You need to plan ahead for your mini cakes just as you do for a large cake (or any time-consuming project!). You may need to make sugar decorations ahead of time, and allow plenty of time to bake the cakes and make the fillings, cut and assemble the cakes, and then decorate. Keep in mind when sculpting mini cakes that they can be difficult to manage because they are not attached to cake bases. Be patient and handle them with care. If you find they are moving too much, tack them down to your turntable or work surface with a dab of Royal Icing or a piece of tape on the bottom of the cake's cardboard.

Mini cakes do offer at least one time and effort saver: You usually do not need to dowel them — mini cakes are small and low enough that you can generally skip this step.

Tomato Mini Cakes

YIELD: 10 MINI CAKES

These tomato plants are such a surprise — they look like tiny potted gardens, but they are really sweet treats. We usually make them with chocolate cake, so it resembles dirt all the way down to the bottom of the pot. This is a great project to make with or for children, as it does not require a lot of work. The little pots can be found at a craft store or you can use small plastic or terra-cotta pots if you line them with aluminum foil. If you want to make these mini cakes for Halloween, skip the sugar tomato and add some gummy worms and candy eyeballs to the dirt instead.

Method

ONE DAY IN ADVANCE: MAKE THE TOMATOES

1.   Divide the fondant and dye 2 pounds of it tomato red and 1 pound moss green.

2.   To make the tomatoes, roll a 2-ounce piece of red fondant into a ball. Using a ball tool or toothpick, make a small indent about ¼ inch deep at the top center of the tomato. Use the back of a paring knife to make about 5 slits along the top and sides of the tomato, to give it a slightly irregular, tomato-like shape.

3.   To make the stems, roll 1 ounce of green fondant into a ball. On a greased plastic mat, use the side of the ball tool to roll and flatten out the sides of the ball. There should be a point in the center and the sides should be thinned, like a sombrero.

4.   Using a paring knife, cut away 6 small triangles from the thinned sides to make the individual sections of the stem (similar to a flower's calyx). Using your fingers, pinch the 6 remaining extensions to give them a rounded look. Pinch the center stem between your fingers and form it into a cylinder for the top of the stem.

5.   Using a brush and a dab of water, attach the stem to the top of the tomato.

ASSEMBLE THE MINI CAKES

1.   Prepare the cake batter and bake in a half-sheet pan as directed in the recipe. Let it cool 20 minutes, remove from the pan, then wrap tightly in plastic wrap and freeze for at least one hour. (This makes the cake easier to cut.)

2.   While the cake is chilling, prepare your pots by lining them with aluminum foil and make the frosting.

3.   Using a 3-inch round cookie cutter, cut out 10 round pieces of cake. Then, using a 2¼-inch cutter, cut out 10 pieces of cake. If you do not have round cutters, use a serrated knife and the top of a round glass. These sizes are only approximate, and the edges of the cake do not need to be perfect because they will be covered with filling.

4.   For each cake, put a dab of frosting in the bottom of the pot and place one 2¼-inch cake round on top. Spread about 2 tablespoons of filling on top of the cake and layer the 3-inch round on top of that. Then frost the top of the cake layer with filling and use a small offset spatula to form a small dome.

5.   Press ½ cup of chocolate wafer crumbs per pot onto the filling and place the sugar tomato on top. If you are planning to travel with these cakes, stick a toothpick into the bottom of the tomato and stick the other end into the cake to prevent the tomato from shifting.

HOT TIP

■ You can also make the tomatoes from marzipan. Color marzipan as you would fondant or gum paste.

Monogram Mini Cakes

YIELD: 15 INDIVIDUAL 3-INCH ROUND CAKES

These are our version of petits fours. Even more elegant and beautiful, they are just a little larger and wonderful for weddings, anniversaries, engagement parties, or birthdays. Decorate them with monograms, initials, a date, or a special symbol (such as a heart, star, or logo). Find your favorite font and use it as a template for your letters. If you have extra time, you can embellish the sides with edible pearls, subtle stripes, or Swiss dots.

What You Need

CAKE

1 cake recipe
(see *Basic Recipes* pages 49–52)

1 frosting recipe (see *Basic Recipes* pages 55–57)

MATERIALS

Shortening (for rolling out gum paste and fondant)

1 pound gum paste

4 pounds fondant
(store-bought or page 60)

Food-coloring gels: rose pink, sky blue, buckeye brown

Gold metallic luster dust (optional)

Lemon extract (optional)

EQUIPMENT

Toothpicks

Plastic mat

Small rolling pin

Cookie cutters or templates for letters

1 piece of parchment paper

Fifteen 3-inch round cardboards or foam core

3-inch round cookie cutter

Scissors

Paring knife or X-acto knife

Small offset spatula

Fondant smoothers

Small paintbrush

Small dish of water

TECHNIQUES

Crumb coating cake (page 33)

Dyeing fondant and gum paste (page 40)

Covering cake with fondant (page 34)

Measuring gum paste and fondant (page 61)

$$A\ B\ C\ D\ E$$
$$F\ G\ H\ I$$
$$J\ K\ L\ M\ N$$
$$O\ P\ Q\ R$$
$$S\ T\ U\ V\ W$$
$$X\ Y\ Z$$

Method

MAKE THE LETTERS

1. Dye the gum paste to your desired colors. On a plastic mat greased with shortening, roll out the gum paste to approximately ⅛ inch thick. Using the cookie cutters of your choice, cut out the letters. For a fancy script look, pinch the ends of each letter.

2. If you have time, let the letters dry on a piece of parchment paper for a few hours. This is not absolutely necessary but will make the letters easier to handle when placing them on the cakes.

MAKE AND ASSEMBLE THE MINI CAKES

1. Prepare the cake batter and bake in a half-sheet pan as directed in the recipe. Let it cool for 20 minutes, remove from the pan, then wrap tightly in plastic wrap and freeze for at least one hour. (This makes the cake easier to cut.)

2. While the cakes are chilling, make the frosting.

3. Cut the cake into fifteen 3-inch rounds.

4. For each cake, place a dab of frosting on each cardboard round and place one cake round on top. Crumb coat the outside of each cake with a very thin layer of frosting.

5. Dye the fondant to your desired colors. In the mini cakes pictured here, we use chocolate fondant for the brown, pale pink fondant, pale blue fondant, and white fondant painted with a mixture of gold metallic luster dust and lemon extract. You will need approximately 4 ounces of fondant per cake.

6. On a greased plastic mat, roll the fondant out to ⅛ inch thick. Cover each cake with rolled fondant. Trim the excess fondant off each cake.

7. Use a dab of water and a brush to moisten the back of the letters and attach them directly on top of the mini cakes.

HOT TIPS

▨ If you want to paint the letters in metallic luster dust (page 17), do so before attaching the letters to the cakes.

▨ If you make the letters days in advance and they harden, they may not stay on the cakes with water alone. Use Royal Icing to attach them.

▨ Display these mini cakes on flattened cupcake wrappers, a cake stand, small lace doilies, or napkins.

Party Hat Mini Cakes

YIELD: 3 INDIVIDUAL CAKES

These adorable, zany, buttercream-covered party hats are sure to put a smile on anyone's face. You can dress them up in bold colors as we did here or customize them in black, white, silver, and gold for a New Year's Eve party. They are a decadent treat — and they do not require a covering of fondant.

What You Need

CAKE

1 cake recipe
(see *Basic Recipes* pages 49–52)

1 Swiss-Meringue Butter-
cream recipe (page 56)

MATERIALS

1½ pounds fondant
(store-bought or page 60)
or gum paste

Shortening (for rolling out
fondant or gum paste)

Food-coloring gels: super red,
electric pink, sunset orange,
sky blue, electric purple,
lemon yellow, royal blue,
leaf green, electric green,
bakers rose

EQUIPMENT

Toothpicks

Plastic mat

Paring knife or X-acto knife

Scissors

Three 3-inch round
cardboard or foam core bases

Round cookie cutters
(2¼ inches, 3½ inches)

Pastry bags and couplers

#10 pastry tip

Small offset spatula

Small serrated knife

Small rolling pin

1-inch round cookie cutter
(optional)

Heart and star cookie cutters
(optional)

Paintbrushes or wooden
dowels (to make sugar
streamers)

Palette knife

TECHNIQUES

Dyeing fondant and
gum paste (page 40)

Filling cake (page 31)

Crumb coating cake
(page 33)

Sculpting cake (page 32)

Filling a pastry bag
(page 38)

Piping dots (page 39)

Party streamers
(optional, page 45)

Measuring gum paste and
fondant (page 61)

Method

MAKE THE DECORATIONS

1.   Divide half (12 ounces) of the fondant or gum paste into three 4-ounce portions. Dye one section lemon yellow, another electric green, and the other sunset orange.

2.   From each color you will need to make 25 balls and one hat topper. On a plastic mat greased with shortening, roll out 3 of the 4 ounces of each color into a long rope, approximately 8 inches long and ¼ inch thick. Use a paring knife to cut each rope into twenty-five ⅜-inch sections. (Reroll the fondant until you have enough pieces.) With lightly greased hands roll the pieces into equal-sized balls.

3.   To make the hat topper, roll each remaining 1 ounce piece of fondant into a ball. Shape the ball into a cone. Stick the points of the cones about halfway onto toothpicks. Pinch the ends of the cones to secure them on the toothpicks. Use scissors to make repeated cuts to create the fringe.

HOT TIP
■ To embellish the look of your party hats, make some festive party streamers (page 45) in a variety of colors.

MAKE AND ASSEMBLE THE MINI CAKES

1. Prepare the cake batter and bake in a half-sheet pan as directed in the recipe. Let it cool for 20 minutes, remove from pan, then wrap tightly in plastic wrap and freeze for at least one hour. (This makes the cake easier to cut.)

2. While the cake is chilling, make the buttercream.

3. Cut the cake into six 3½-inch rounds and six 2¼-inch rounds.

4. Place a dab of buttercream on each cardboard, then place one layer of the 3½-inch round cake on top of the buttercream. Coat the first layer with ½ inch of buttercream and place the next 3½-inch round layer on top. Repeat this method with two of the 2¼-inch rounds. In the end you will have four layers of cake and three layers of filling. After the top layer of cake is on, push down slightly to secure the layers. Place the stacks in the freezer until they're hard to the touch, approximately 1 hour.

5. Using a serrated knife, carve each cake into a cone shape. Start carving at the top and work your way down to the bottom. Crumb coat the cakes with a very thin layer of filling.

6. Mix the buttercream colors you plan to use. For the hats pictured we used blue, purple, and pink. Put each color into a pastry bag fitted with a #10 tip.

7. Pipe dots of buttercream all over each cake, with no spaces in between. Start at the bottom of the cake and stagger the dots until you reach the top of the hat.

8. Use a clean toothpick to make a hole in the very top of the hat. This allows the topper (on its own toothpick) to slide right into the cake. Place the topper on the cake.

9. Divide the remaining 12 ounces of fondant or gum paste into three 4-ounce pieces and dye the colors for the heart, star, and circle decorations pictured.

10. On a plastic mat greased with shortening, roll out the gum paste to ⅛ inch thick. Cut out the various designs using shaped cutters. You need approximately 10 decorations for each hat. Place the shapes in a scattered pattern right onto the buttercream, being careful not to press too hard or they will ruin your piped pattern.

11. Carefully transfer the cake to the plate or tray on which you plan to serve it. Press the fondant balls lightly into the buttercream around the bottom of the cake, with no spaces in between.

Dice Mini Cakes

YIELD: 4 INDIVIDUAL CAKES

I love making cakes that re-create everyday objects. These cakes remind me of those fuzzy dice you would see hanging from a car's rearview mirror in the fifties. Make them in any color combination you like. They are perfect for the high roller in your life.

Method

1. Prepare the cake batter and bake in a half-sheet pan as directed in the recipe. Let it cool for 20 minutes, remove from pans, then wrap tightly in plastic wrap and freeze for at least one hour. (This makes the cake easier to cut.)

2. While the cakes are chilling, make the frosting.

3. Cut the cake into twelve 3½ x 3½-inch squares.

4. For each cake, place a dab of filling on each cardboard square and place a square of cake on top of the filling. Coat the first layer with ½ inch of filling. Top the filling with another square, coat those squares, and place the remaining squares on top. In the end you will have 3 layers of cake with 2 layers of filling. After the top layer of cake is on, push down slightly to secure the layers. Place the cakes in the freezer and chill for 1 hour.

5. Using a serrated knife, carefully cut away slivers of cake to create a slightly rounded effect on all edges of the cake. Start with the top edges then work on the side edges, then along the bottom. Trim the cardboard so it doesn't show. Crumb coat the cakes with a very thin layer of filling.

6. Divide the fondant into 4 equal portions, and dye the fondant in your desired colors.

7. On a plastic mat greased with shortening, roll out the fondant to ¼ inch thick. Cover each cake with fondant. Even though these cakes are squares, do not pinch the corners, because you want the cakes to have the rounded edges that you find on actual dice.

8. For the dots color 4 ounces of gum paste in the colors you want to use. On a plastic mat greased with shortening, roll out the gum paste to ⅟₁₆ inch thick. Use a #806 tip or a ½-inch round cutter to cut out 20 dots for each cake.

9. Use a dab of water to moisten the dots slightly and attach them to the cake.

HOT TIP

To make a realistic-looking cake, refer to real dice when rounding the edges and attaching the dots.

What You Need

CAKE

1 cake recipe
(see *Basic Recipes* pages 49–52)

1 frosting recipe
(see *Basic Recipes* pages 55–57)

MATERIALS

8 pounds fondant (store-bought or page 60)

Food-coloring gels: super red, egg yellow, black

Shortening (for rolling out gum paste)

¼ pound gum paste

Cornstarch (for rolling out fondant)

EQUIPMENT

Four 3½ x 3½-inch cardboard or foam core squares

Small serrated knife

Ruler

Small offset spatula

Toothpicks

Large rolling pin

Strainer

Dry pastry brush

Paring knife or X-acto knife

Fondant smoothers

Plastic mat

Small rolling pin

#806 pastry tip or a ½-inch round cutter

Small paintbrush

Small dish of water

TECHNIQUES

Filling cake (page 31)

Sculpting cakes (page 32)

Crumb coating cake (page 33)

Dyeing fondant and gum paste (page 40)

Covering cake with fondant (page 34)

Mini Present Cakes

YIELD: 4 INDIVIDUAL CAKES

One of the most popular cakes we do at Confetti Cakes, **mini presents are simple and absolutely adorable.** We made them for one wedding and all the guests thought they were the favors to take home — they looked just like real gift boxes. These are perfect for bridal and baby showers, weddings, birthdays, or any holiday. Make them orange and black for Halloween, pink and red for Valentine's Day, or red and green for Christmas. You can dress them up with colorful bows, monograms, stripes, or polka dots or make them super sophisti-cated with metallic colors or tone-on-tone designs.

What You Need

CAKE

1 cake recipe (see *Basic Recipes* pages 49–52)

1 frosting recipe (*Basic Recipes* pages 55–57)

½ recipe Royal Icing (page 58)

MATERIALS

2 pounds gum paste

Shortening (for rolling out gum paste)

2 pounds fondant (store-bought or page 60)

Food-coloring gels: bakers rose, lemon yellow, willow green

Cornstarch (for rolling out fondant)

EQUIPMENT

Plastic mat

Small rolling pin

Ruler

Paring knife or X-acto knife

Paper towels

Four 3 x 3-inch cardboard or foam core squares

Small serrated knife

Small offset spatula

Toothpicks

Large rolling pin

Strainer

Dry pastry brush

Fondant smoothers

pastry tips #12, #2

Pastry bag and coupler

Small paintbrush

Small dish of water

TECHNIQUES

Sugar bows and ribbons (page 44)

Filling cake (page 31)

Crumb coating cake (page 33)

Dyeing fondant and gum paste (page 40)

Covering cake with fondant (page 34)

Measuring gum paste and fondant (page 61)

Method

TWO DAYS IN ADVANCE: MAKE THE BOWS

Following the instructions on page 44, make four gum-paste bows and ribbon tails to fit the 3 x 3-inch present cakes.

MAKE AND ASSEMBLE THE MINI CAKES

1. Prepare the cake batter and bake in a half-sheet pan as directed in the recipe. Let it cool for 20 minutes, remove from pan, then wrap tightly in plastic wrap and freeze for at least one hour. (This makes the cake easier to cut.)

2. While the cakes are chilling, make the frosting and Royal Icing.

3. Cut the cake into eight 3 x 3-inch squares. For each cake, place a dab of Royal Icing on each cardboard square and place a square of cake on top of that.

4. Coat the bottom layer with approximately ½ inch of filling and place the remaining square on top. Each cake consists of 2 layers of cake and 1 layer of filling. After the top layer of cake is on, push down slightly to secure the layers. Place the cakes in the freezer and chill for 1 hour.

5. Make sure the edges are completely even by trimming with a serrated knife. Cut away any cardboard that is showing either with a serrated knife or scissors. Crumb coat each cake with a very thin layer of filling.

6. Dye the fondant in your desired colors. For the cakes pictured here, we used pale pink, pale green, and pale yellow. You'll use approximately 8 ounces for each cake.

7. On a surface dusted with cornstarch, roll out the fondant to ¼ inch thick. Cover each cake with rolled fondant and trim.

8. On a plastic mat greased with shortening, roll out the remaining gum paste (you will have already used some to make the bows ahead of time) to approximately ⅛ inch thick and cut into ½ x 8-inch strips.

9. Using water and a brush, moisten the strips slightly and attach them to the fondant-covered cakes. There should be two strips on each cake, perpendicular to one another making a cross in the top center, like ribbon tied around a box.

10. To attach the sugar bows, glue the two tails in the center of the top of the present with Royal Icing, and then attach the bow on top of where the tails cross.

11. If you would like to add polka dots, roll out any remaining gum paste to approximately ⅛ inch thick and, using a pastry tip, cut out the size polka dots you desire. For the cakes in the photo we used a #12 tip. Moisten the backs of the dots with a dab of water and affix to the cake.

HOT TIP

■ If you want to paint the ribbon with metallic powders, **do so before attaching them** to the cakes so you don't get powder all over the cakes.

Retro Television Mini Cakes

I created this cake with my brother Eric in mind. He works in the television industry and is a computer whiz who can fix anything electronic. If it were not for him, I would probably still have a television that looks like this!

What You Need

CAKE

1 cake recipe (see *Basic Recipes* pages 49–52)

1 frosting recipe (see *Basic Recipes* pages 55–57)

MATERIALS

2 pounds fondant

Cornstarch (for rolling out fondant)

Food-coloring gels: buckeye brown, coal black

½ pound gum paste

Shortening (for rolling out gum paste)

Silver metallic luster dust

Lemon extract

EQUIPMENT

Four 4 x 2½-inch cardboard or foam core rectangles

Paring knife or X-acto knife

Ruler

Small serrated knife

Small offset spatula

Toothpicks

Large rolling pin

Strainer

Dry pastry brush

Fondant smoothers

Medium paintbrush with stiff bristles

Small dish of water

Plastic mat

Small rolling pin

Pastry tips: #10, #12, #806 (or a ½-inch round cutter)

Two 18-inch cloth-covered wires (available in cake-decorating stores)

Scissors

2 small paintbrushes

TECHNIQUES

Filling cake (page 31)

Wood staining (page 42)

Crumb coating cake (page 33)

Dyeing fondant and gum paste (page 40)

Covering cake with fondant (page 40)

Measuring gum paste and fondant (page 61)

Method

1. Prepare the cake batter and bake in a half-sheet pan as directed in the recipe. Let it cool for 20 minutes, remove from pan, then wrap lightly in plastic wrap and freeze for at least one hour. (This will make the cake easier to cut.)

2. While the cake is chilling, make the frosting.

3. Cut the cake into twelve 4 x 2½-inch rectangles.

4. For each cake, place a dab of filling on each cardboard rectangle and place a piece of cake on top. Coat the bottom layers with ½ inch of filling. Top the filling with another piece of cake, add another ½ inch of filling, then the final set of cake layers. In the end you will have three layers of cake with two layers of filling. After the top layer of cake is on, push down slightly to secure the layers. Place the cakes in the freezer and chill for 1 hour.

5. Using a serrated knife, carefully trim the sides of the cake to make it a rectangle approximately 4 inches wide, 3½ inches high, and 2½ inches deep. For the screen, starting ¼ inch in from the left outer edge of the cake, measure a rectangle that is 3 inches wide and 2½ inches high. Use a toothpick or the tip of a paring knife to mark this rectangle. Carefully cut straight on all the edges, leaving the area a little rounded in the middle. Crumb coat the cakes with a very thin layer of filling. Be extra careful around the screen area so you do not lose any definition.

6. Prepare 2 pounds of fondant, ½ pound for each cake, using the wood-staining technique. On a surface dusted with cornstarch, roll the fondant out to ¼ inch thick and cover each cake. Paint the entire cake, except for the screen, with the wood-staining technique.

7. To make the speakers and knobs, dye 4 ounces of gum paste black. On a plastic mat greased with shortening, roll the gum paste out to ⅛ inch thick. Cut it into four ½ x 1-inch rectangles that will be placed on the lower right-hand side of the cakes. Using your paring knife, make a few horizontal slits in the black gum paste to give it texture, being careful not to cut completely through it.

8. Roll out about half of the remaining gum paste to ⅛ inch thick. Use a round #806 tube to cut out 8 large dots. Cut out the centers of these dots with the #12 tip to create rings. Cut two small rectangles to fit into the centers of the rings. You will need 2 rings and 2 rectangles for each TV. Set them aside.

9. With the same gum paste, use a #10 tip to cut out 8 dots to be placed above the television knobs. Set them aside.

10. To make the antenna bases, roll out gum paste into two small balls the size of marbles, approximately ¾ inch in diameter each. Using a paring knife, cut these balls in half so the flat bottom can be placed on top of the televisions. You will get two antenna bases from each ball.

11. Paint the screens, knobs, and antenna bases silver with the silver luster dust mixed with lemon extract.

12. To make the antennas, cut each cloth-covered wire into four pieces, approximately 4 inches each. Attach a tiny ball of gum paste with water to the top of each wire to form an antenna. Paint both the wires and the balls silver. Stick two wires directly into the antenna base, placing them at angles.

13. Refer to the photo for proper placement. Using a brush moistened with water, attach all the decorations to the cake.

What You Need

CAKE

1 cake recipe
(see *Basic Recipes* pages 49–52)

1 filling recipe (See *Basic Recipes* pages 55–57)

½ recipe Royal Icing (page 58)

MATERIALS

4 pounds gum paste

Food-coloring gels:
super red, lemon yellow

Shortening (for rolling out gum paste)

Small dish of water

2 small paintbrushes

Powdered food coloring:
brown, yellow (optional)

Medium paintbrush

4 pounds fondant
(store-bought or page 60)

Cornstarch (for rolling out fondant)

EQUIPMENT

Toothpicks

Plastic mat

Paring knife or X-acto knife

Ruler

Ball tool

Small brushes

Small dish of water

Four 4 x 2½-inch cardboard or foam core rectangles

Scissors

Small serrated knife

Small offset spatula

Large rolling pin

Strainer

Dry pastry brush

Fondant smoothers

Small rolling pin

Pastry bag and coupler

#2 pastry tip

TECHNIQUES

Dyeing fondant and gum paste (page 40)

Filling cake (page 31)

Crumb coating cake (page 33)

Piecing fondant (page 36)

Measuring gum paste and fondant (page 61)

Popcorn Mini Cakes

YIELD: 4 INDIVIDUAL CAKES

These little bags make my dad laugh. He can make an entire meal out of popcorn. He loves it. No matter what time of day my family ends up at a movie theater, even if we just came from dinner — no movie is complete without a bag of popcorn. I adore these old-fashioned popcorn bags. We like to create them out of buttery vanilla cake. It is the perfect dessert for a movie buff, Oscar night, or a birthday party. No one will believe that the kernels of popped corn are actually made out of sugar!

Method

ONE DAY IN ADVANCE: MAKE THE POPCORN KERNELS

For each cake you need approximately 20 kernels of sugar popcorn.

1.   Dye 2 pounds of the gum paste butter yellow.

2.   On a plastic mat greased with shortening, roll the butter yellow gum paste out into a long rope approximately 10 inches long and ½ inch thick.

3.   Using a paring knife, cut the rope at various intervals. Cut twenty half-inch pieces, twenty quarter-inch pieces, and twenty eighth-inch pieces. With greased hands, roll all the pieces into balls. Repeat with 3 more ropes of gum paste.

4.   Use the small end of a ball tool to create ¼-inch-deep indents in the half-inch balls. Create ⅛-inch-deep indents in

the smaller pieces. Use your fingers to give the edges a little misshaping, pinching the sides into the shape of a human ear. You do not want anything to look too perfect. Popcorn comes in all shapes and sizes.

5.   Attach one half-inch ball and one quarter-inch ball using a dab of water, sticking the smooth sides together and pointing the indents toward the outside. Then attach one of the eighth-inch pieces to the first two with a dab of water to create one piece of popcorn. Repeat the process for the rest of the popcorn. Feel free to add more balls to some kernels and just one ball to others to create the irregular look you'd find in real popcorn.

6.   With a dry brush, dust on a dab of yellow powder, to add a light shade of butter. In a small dish, mix together water and brown food-coloring powder to make a very subtle shade of brown and paint the centers of all the indents to create the actual look of kernels.

MAKE AND ASSEMBLE THE MINI CAKES

1. Prepare the cake batter and bake in a half-sheet pan as directed in the recipe. Let it cool for 20 minutes, remove from pan, then wrap tightly in plastic wrap and freeze for at least one hour. (This makes the cake easier to cut.)

2. While the cakes are chilling, make the filling and Royal Icing.

3. Cut the cake into twelve 4 x 2½-inch rectangles.

4. For each cake, place a dab of filling on each cardboard rectangle and place a piece of cake on top. Coat the first layer with ½ inch of filling. Top the filling with another piece of cake, coat again with another ½ inch of filling, then place remaining piece of cake on top. In the end you will have 3 layers of cake with 2 layers of filling. After the top layer of cake is on, push down slightly to secure the layers. Place the cakes in a freezer and chill for 1 hour.

5. Using a serrated knife, carve a gusset into the sides of the cakes (this is the upside-down Y shape that is found on the sides of brown paper bags and shopping bags that allows them to fold neatly). To assist in the carving process, refer to a real shopping bag. Crumb coat the cakes with a very thin layer of filling.

6. On a surface dusted with cornstarch, roll out 1 pound of white fondant to approximately ⅛ inch thick for each cake. Using a ruler, cut two 4½ x 4½-inch pieces and two 3 x 4½-inch pieces. Keep the cut pieces covered with a piece of plastic wrap and a damp cloth to prevent them from drying out while you roll out the fondant.

7. For each cake, place the two 4½ x 4½-inch pieces on the front and back sides of the cake, making sure the fondant extends at least ¼ inch above the top of the cake for the bag's opening. (You will not be covering the top of the cake. The popcorn will sit inside the rim you create.) The fondant should also reach at least ¼ inch beyond the sides of the bag. Trim the fondant along the bottom edge of the cake to create a clean edge.

8. Brush the fondant that extends past the sides of the cake with a dab of water, then place the 3 x 4½-inch pieces against the sides of the cake. Pinch the fondant pieces together at the seams of the bag, and press it into the gussets that you carved in step 4. If the seams do not look clean, use a scissors to cut away the excess fondant.

9. Dye the remaining 2 pounds of gum paste red. On a plastic mat greased with shortening, roll out the gum paste to ¹⁄₁₆ inch thick and cut it into fourteen ³⁄₈ x 4½-inch strips for each bag. Moisten the backs of the strips with a dab of water and attach them to the cake at even intervals. Fold the tops of the strips over the top edge of the fondant. For even spacing, place a ruler along the bottom edge of the cake as your guide. Red-colored gum paste tends to bleed, so try not to apply too much water to the backs of the red strips or the color may bleed into the white background.

10. Use a pastry bag filled with Royal Icing to adhere the popcorn pieces inside the bag and along the outside edge. Have a few pieces positioned to look like they are literally ready to fall off the edge, but use the icing to make sure they don't!

HOT TIPS

■ Since you will be making a large quantity of popcorn, keep the gum paste you are not using covered at all times in plastic wrap. Roll out small amounts at a time to prevent the gum paste from drying out. Ideally, you'll make about 20 pieces at a time.

■ Use kernels of real popcorn as your inspiration.

■ Everyone loves the combination of sweet and salty, so if you want to save time, use real popcorn instead of sugar popcorn.

■ Make tiny popcorn buckets out of cupcakes so you do not have to sculpt cakes or make as much popcorn. Just wrap one piece of fondant around the cupcake's outer edge and fill with popcorn.

Tote Bag Mini Cakes

YIELD: 4 INDIVIDUAL CAKES

I am always carrying things back and forth between my bakery and home. One year for my birthday my friends Alison and Jeremy decided to buy me a fabulous pink tote bag, with my name on it. I thought it would be adorable to make it out of cake. The one pictured here has their monogram on it. Note that these cakes should be made one day in advance of serving, to let the handle dry. Refer to the illustration for details.

Method

1. Prepare the cake batter and bake in a half-sheet pan as directed in the recipe. Let it cool for 20 minutes, remove from pan, then wrap tightly in plastic wrap and freeze for at least one hour. (This makes the cake easier to cut.)

2. While the cake is chilling, make the frosting.

3. Cut the cake into twelve 4 x 3-inch squares.

4. For each cake, place a dab of filling on each shaped cardboard and place a square of cake on top. Coat the square with ½ inch of filling, top the filling with another square, coat with another ½ inch of filling, and place the last square on top. In the end you will have 3 layers of cake with 2 layers of filling. After the top layer of cake is on, push down slightly to secure the layers.

Place the cakes in the freezer and chill for 1 hour.

5. Using a serrated knife, carefully cut away slivers of cake to create the rounded sides of the tote bag. Cut away small amounts of the cake at the base so that the bottom curves under slightly, like a real bag. The top of the cakes should look more like an elongated oval. Crumb coat the cakes with a very thin layer of filling.

6. Dye all of the fondant a light shade of ivory using a touch of the brown gel. On a greased plastic mat, roll out a large piece to ⅛ inch thick and cover the rest in plastic wrap. See the illustrations on page 145 for these step-by-step instructions. (A) Cut one piece in the shape of an oval for the top of the cake, approximately 2½ inches wide and 4 inches long. (B) Cut two pieces for the

What You Need

CAKE

1 cake recipe
(see *Basic Recipes* pages 49–52)

1 frosting recipe (see *Basic Recipes* pages 55–57)

MATERIALS

2 pounds fondant (store-bought or page 60)

Cornstarch (for rolling out fondant)

Food-coloring gels: super brown, sky blue

Lemon extract

Silver luster dust

1 pound gum paste

Shortening (for rolling out gum paste)

EQUIPMENT

Four 3½ x 2½-inch cardboard or foam core rectangles with the edges rounded at the corners (bases are cut slightly smaller than the cake so you will not need to cut again)

Small serrated knife

Ruler

Paring knife or X-acto knife

Small offset spatula

Toothpicks

Plastic mat

Small rolling pin

Fondant smoothers

Stitching tool

2 small paintbrushes

Small dish of water

TECHNIQUES

Filling cake (page 31)

Crumb coating cake (page 33)

Sculpting cake (page 32)

Dyeing fondant and gum paste (page 40)

Piecing fondant (page 36)

Measuring gum paste and fondant (page 61)

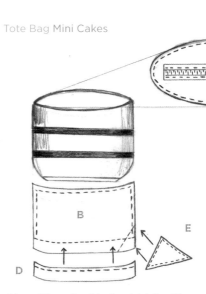

C

A

B

E

D

10. To make the straps, dye the gum paste blue (or the color of your choice). On a plastic mat greased with shortening, roll out the gum paste to ⅛ inch thick. Use the ruler and paring knife or scalpel to cut out two ½ inch x 6-inch strips for the bottom of the bag, two ⅜ inch x 10-inch strips for the handles, and two triangles that measure 2 inches on the bottom and 1½ inches on the other sides. Repeat for each cake.

11. (D) Use a brush to moisten the gum-paste strips with a dab of water. For each cake, attach two strips to the bottom of bag and have them meet at the seams created by the fondant. Add stitch marks along the top of the strips.

12. (E) Attach the triangles to each side of each bag with a dab of water. Add stitch marks along the triangle edges after you place them on the bag.

13. (F) To make the handles, first lay the strips down and make the stitch marks along the sides of each edge. Then flip the strips over and moisten approximately 2 inches of each end on each strip. For each cake, attach one end to the left of the center of the bag, placing it right up against the blue bottom strip. Attach the other end of the strip on the same side, to the right of the center of the bag. This should leave some slack in the middle of the handle. Place a rolled-up piece of paper toweling through the handles so they keep their shape as they dry. Repeat on the other side. Let the handles dry for at least a day (more if it's humid) then pull the toweling away and they will stand on their own.

14. For the monogram, cut out tiny letters from gum paste and attach them with a dab of water, or write on the cake with edible food markers.

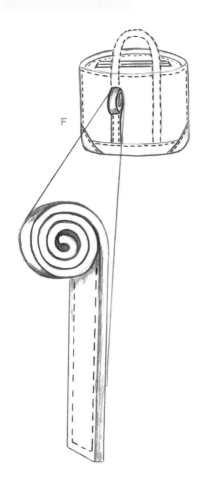

F

sides of the cake, 4 inches high by 6½ inches wide. The sides should be extra wide so there is room to overlap the two pieces. Work on one cake at a time.

7. With a brush, moisten the edges of the oval fondant shape with water. For each cake, wrap one of the side pieces around the cake, making sure to cover the edge of the top oval. Attach the second piece, starting on one side of the cake, in the middle, where the tote's side seam will go. Use a dab of water to tack it down to hold it in place while you wrap the piece around the body of the cake. Brush a dab of water on that side to hold it in place. If the fondant is too wide (if it stretches past where the seam should be), trim it to fit.

8. Soon after the fondant pieces are applied (no longer than 30 minutes), use the stitching tool (or the end of a toothpick) to make stitch marks along the two sides of the cake, to create the side seams. Then run the stitching tool around the top oval of the cake, as close to the top edge as you can.

9. (C) To make the zippers, make a rectangular box with stitching marks down the center on the top of the cake, using a scalpel or a thin blade. Make the teeth of the zipper with a series of lines placed close to one another inside the long rectangular box. Mix a bit of lemon extract and silver dust and use a very small brush to paint the zipper silver.

Mini Wedding Cakes

YIELD: 3 INDIVIDUAL CAKES

These are beautiful, elegant tiered cakes, only in miniature. Each of the three designs pictured has a special style. One has a funky flair, another a delicate touch of pearls, and the third is reminiscent of a starry night. These make an eye-catching dessert for any special occasion. Make them look bridal for a shower or whimsical for a Sunday tea. I think they are just so precious!

Method

ONE DAY (OR UP TO A WEEK) IN ADVANCE: MAKE THE DECORATIONS

Leaves

1. Dye 2 ounces of gum paste lime green.

2. On a plastic mat greased with shortening, roll out the lime green gum paste to $\frac{1}{16}$ inch thick. Using the leaf cutter, cut out 9 leaves. Place each leaf into a leaf-veiner mold, make the vein impression, and place them in the bottoms of a clean egg carton to dry. Make sure one end of each leaf remains flat; this will make it easier to attach the leaves to the cakes.

Rose (illustration A, page 151)

1. Dye 2 ounces of gum paste orange.

2. For the center of the rose, on a plastic mat greased with shortening, roll 1 marble-sized ball of gum paste, approximately $\frac{1}{2}$ inch in diameter, and shape it into a cone. For the petals, roll out the remaining gum paste to $\frac{1}{16}$ inch thick. Using the large petal cutter, cut out 13 to 15 rose petals. Place one petal in the palm of your hand and use the large end of a ball tool to thin the edges. Slightly moisten the inside of one petal and wrap it around the top of the cone to form the inside bud. Thin the edges of the next three petals with the ball tool and apply them to the rose in an overlapping pattern. Next, thin and add a ring of five petals. As you go, pull the tops of the petals away from the center to give the rose some shape. Add extra petals to fill it out.

3. To help the rose hold its shape as it dries, place some crumpled paper towels around the edges to support the petals. Let the rose dry overnight then dust the edges of the petals slightly with a dry brush and red food-coloring powder.

Dogwood Petals (illustration B, page 151)

1. Dye 2 ounces of gum paste purple and 1 ounce of gum paste lilac.

2. On a plastic mat greased with shortening, roll out the purple gum paste to $\frac{1}{16}$ inch thick. Using the dogwood cutter, cut out 3 full flowers. Divide these in quarters, giving you

What You Need

CAKE

1 cake recipe (see *Basic Recipes* pages 49–52)

1 frosting recipe (see *Basic Recipes* pages 55–57)

1 recipe Royal Icing (page 58)

MATERIALS

1½ pounds gum paste

Shortening (for rolling out gum paste)

Food-coloring gels: sunset orange, electric pink, regal purple, leaf green, lemon yellow

Powdered food coloring: orange, purple, red, lime green, green

Pearl luster dust

Decorations: edible pearls, gold nonpareils (available in cake-decorating stores)

3 pounds fondant (store-bought or page 60)

Cornstarch (for rolling out fondant)

EQUIPMENT

Toothpicks

Plastic mat

Small rolling pin

Gum-paste cutters: large, medium, and small rose petal cutters; dogwood cutter; leaf cutter

Leaf-veiner mold

Egg carton

Ball tool

Paper towels

Palette knife

Cardboard to go under each layer of cake **BEFORE** stacking: three 4-inch rounds, three 3-inch rounds, three 2-inch rounds

Three 5-inch round foam core bases

Large rolling pin

Strainer

Dry pastry brush

Fondant smoothers

Ruler

Paring knife or X-acto knife

Small serrated knife

Small offset spatula

Pastry bag and coupler

Pastry tips: #2, #10 (to cut out polka dots)

3 small paintbrushes

Small dish of water

Tweezers

Decorative ribbon (for cake bases)

White glue (for decorative ribbon)

Scissors

TECHNIQUES

Covering cake base with fondant (page 36)

Splitting cake (page 29)

Filling cake (page 31)

Crumb coating cake (page 33)

Covering cake in fondant (page 34)

Dyeing fondant and gum paste (page 40)

Measuring gum paste and fondant (page 61)

---

4 petals from each flower, or a total of 12 petals. Place one petal in the palm of your hand and use the large end of a ball tool to thin the edges. Let the petals dry in a clean egg carton to help the petals hold a slightly cupped shape. Once the petals are dry and firm, dust the edges slightly with a dry brush and purple powder.

Whimsical Dahlia (illustration C)

1. Dye 4 ounces of gum paste fuchsia.

2. On a plastic mat greased with shortening, roll out the fuchsia gum paste to 1/16 inch thick. Using the medium and small cutters, cut out 8 medium petals and 12 small petals. Overlap and pinch the rounded side of these petals, leaving the sharp point on the outside and pinching the other end in the shape of a cone. Let the petals dry overnight. Dust the petals with red and orange powder.

MAKE AND ASSEMBLE THE MINI CAKES

1. Prepare the cake batter and bake in a half-sheet pan as directed in the recipe. Let it cool for 20 minutes, remove from pan, then wrap tightly in plastic wrap and freeze for at least one hour. (This makes the cake easier to cut.)

2. While the cake is chilling, make the frosting and the Royal Icing.

3. Cover the cake bases in rolled fondant. Roll out ½ pound of white fondant to ⅛ inch thick. Brush a little water or piping gel on the base and cover them with the fondant. Trim any excess fondant and knead it back into a ball.

4. Cut the cake into three 4-inch rounds, three 3-inch rounds, and three 2-inch rounds. For each cake, place a dab of filling on each cardboard round and place a layer of cake on its corresponding cardboard size (the 4-inch round cakes should go on the 4-inch round cardboard bases and so forth).

5. Split each layer of cake in half with a serrated knife. Coat the bottom half with ¼ inch of filling and replace the top half. Each tier should be approximately 1¼ inches high. Crumb coat the outside of each tier with a very thin layer of filling.

6. On a surface dusted with cornstarch, roll out 1 pound of fondant to ¼ inch thick. Cut out a 7-inch-diameter circle of fondant and cover the bottom tier of the cake. Follow the same process for the other two tiers, using 6-inch and 5-inch circles of fondant.

HOT TIP

■ Since you will be making many decorations, **keep the gum paste you are not using covered in plastic wrap.** Roll out small amounts at a time to prevent it from drying out. It would be a good idea to make the flowers with many petals a few at a time.

7. For each cake, place a dab of Royal Icing onto the fondant-covered base affix the 4-inch round cake onto. Place a dab of Royal Icing in the middle of the bottom tier and place the 3-inch round tier on top of that, and repeat with the 2-inch round tier. Make sure each one is centered before adding the next. (There is no need for dowels since this is a small cake.)

8. Decorate the cakes as desired. As a finishing touch, glue decorative ribbon around each cake base.

Techniques for Cakes Pictured

POLKA DOTS AND ROSE: Pipe a border around the base of each tier with white Royal Icing and a #2 tip. Roll out ½ ounce of fuchsia gum paste to ¹⁄₁₆ inch thick on a plastic mat greased with shortening. Use a #10 tip to cut out approximately 60 polka dots. Using a palette knife, pick each polka dot up and moisten it with a dab of water. Attach the dots in a scattered pattern all over the cake. Using icing, attach 3 leaves to the top of the cake and the rose on top of the leaves.

GOLD NONPAREILS AND DOGWOOD PETALS: Brush the entire cake with water and use tweezers to place the nonpareils all over the cake, one at a time. Using icing, attach 3 leaves on top of the cake.

Form a ¾-inch-diameter ball of lilac gum paste and flatten the bottom slightly to form a dome. Using icing, attach 5 or 6 petals, arranged in a flat ring, to the top of the cake. Use icing to attach the flattened ball in the middle of the petals. Attach the remaining petals with icing, overlapping them if you have to fill in any remaining holes. Make 30 tiny balls, approximately ¼ inch in diameter, out of the remaining lilac gum paste. Moisten the balls with water and attach to the center dome.

PEARLS AND WHIMSICAL DAHLIA: Edible pearls are available at cake-decorating stores, or you can make them. Roll gum paste into little balls and let dry overnight. Shake the balls in pearl luster in a container with a tight-fitting lid, then put them in a strainer to remove the excess dust. Attach the pearls to the cake using tweezers and icing.

Using icing, attach 3 leaves to the top of the cake. Form a ½-inch-diameter ball of fuchsia gum paste, flatten the bottom slightly to form a dome, and attach to the top of the cake with a dab of water. Starting with the medium petals, carefully insert them in a ring around the bottom of the center ball. After all the medium petals are inserted, fill in the flower with the smaller petals.

Teacup Mini Cakes

YIELD: 4 INDIVIDUAL CAKES

Our clients constantly request these precious little teacups and saucers. They are perfect for showers, tea parties, and birthdays. They have tons of little details — even the teacup handle and saucer are made of sugar — and require quite a bit of time and patience, but the results are breathtaking.

What You Need

CAKE

1 cake recipe (see *Basic Recipes* pages 49–52)

1 frosting recipe (see *Basic Recipes* pages 55–57)

1 recipe Royal Icing (page 58)

MATERIALS

2 pounds gum paste

Shortening (for rolling out gum paste and to coat the sugar mold)

Food-coloring gels: bakers rose, leaf green, lemon yellow, sky blue, buckeye brown

2 pounds fondant (store-bought or page 60)

Cornstarch (for rolling out fondant)

¼ cup vodka (for painting)

Sugar cubes (optional)

EQUIPMENT

Plastic mat

Small rolling pin

Ring cutters (4½ inches, 3½ inches, 1¾ inches)

4 teacup saucers, at least 4½ inches in diameter, with the inset circle approximately 2 inches wide (to be used as a mold for your sugar saucers)

Palette knife

Toothpicks

Paring knife or X-acto knife

Four 1½-inch round cardboard or foam core bases

Small offset spatula

Small serrated knife

Ruler

Large rolling pin

Strainer

Dry pastry brush

Fondant smoothers

Pastry bags and couplers

Pastry tips: #2 and #3

Small paintbrush

Small dish of water

TECHNIQUES

Dyeing fondant and gum paste (page 40)

Filling cake (page 31)

Sculpting cake (page 32)

Crumb coating cake (page 33)

Covering cake with fondant (page 34)

Dyeing Royal Icing (page 40)

Piping dots and straight lines (page 39)

Brush embroidery (page 43)

Measuring gum paste and fondant (page 61)

Method

1. **Make the saucers.** On a plastic mat greased with shortening, roll out 3 ounces of white gum paste to ⅛ inch thick for each saucer. Using the 4½-inch cutter, cut out a circle. Use a paring knife to smooth the edges. Coat a saucer with a generous amount of shortening and lay the gum-paste circle onto the saucer and run your fingers along the surface to make sure it is pushed into the indent in the middle of the saucer. Let the saucers dry in a low-humidity space for two days. Insert a palette knife between the gum paste and saucer to release it from the dish. Let it dry for a day after it has been removed from the mold.

2. For the handles and bases, separate 4 ounces of gum paste into 4 portions and dye each portion in pastel colors. On a plastic mat greased with shortening, roll out the gum paste to ¼ inch thick. See the illustrations on page 155 for these step-by-step instructions. (A) Use a 1¾-inch ring to cut out a circle and set it aside. Continue to roll the gum paste out to ⅛ inch thick and cut a ¼-inch x 4-inch strip. Roll up the remaining gum paste, wrap it in plastic, and save it for later. Repeat the process with the remaining 3 portions.

3. (B) Coat your fingers with a bit of shortening and rub around the outside edge of the circle base to make it rounded and smooth. Use a paring knife to score decorative slits all around the circle at ⅛-inch intervals.

4. (C) Coat your fingers again and round the edges of the strip on both sides to remove the sharp edge left by the cutter. (D) Either photocopy or trace the handle template (page 155). Tape the template onto a flat surface. (E) Lay the gum-paste strip on its side to form the shape of the handle. Set aside to dry for at least two days.

1. Prepare the cake batter and bake in a half-sheet pan as directed in the recipe. Let it cool for 20 minutes, remove from pan, then wrap tightly in plastic wrap and freeze for at least one hour. (This makes the cake easier to cut.)

2. While the cakes are chilling, make the frosting and Royal Icing.

3. Cut the cake into eight 3½-inch rounds.

4. For each cake, place a dab of filling on each cardboard round and place a round of cake on top. Coat each cake with ½ inch of filling. Top the filling with another cake round. In the end you will have 2 layers of cake with 1 layer of filling. After the top layer of cake is on, push down slightly to secure the layers. Place the cakes in a freezer and chill for 1 hour.

5. (F) Using a serrated knife, carve away at the sides of the cake, making the edges of the cake slope like a teacup. Use the illustration (page 155) as a guide. Crumb coat the cakes with a very thin layer of filling.

6. For each cake, roll out 8 ounces of white fondant to ¼ inch thick. Cover each cake with white rolled fondant. Make sure the bottom edges of the cakes are completely flat and smooth.

7. (G) Roll out the remaining dyed gum paste to ¼ inch thick and cut a ¼-inch by 8½-inch strip for each cake. Coat your fingers with a bit of shortening and smooth the edges of the strip.

8. (H) Use a brush to moisten the back of the strip with water and attach it around the top edge of the teacups, forming a ring that will serve as the top lip of the cup.

9. (I) Using Royal Icing as your glue, attach the cakes to the sugar bases. (The cake is affixed to the cardboard.) Attach the handles to the side of the cups with 2 dabs of icing (use a toothpick to remove any excess), then attach the entire cake to the saucer.

10. Mix a tiny drop of brown gel with ¼ cup of vodka in a small dish and paint the cake tops in swirling motions, creating streaks that might appear in a real cup of tea.

11. Divide the icing equally among four containers and dye the different portions pale pink, pale yellow, pale green, and pale blue. (These are the colors we used here but feel free to make up your own combinations.)

12. Use piping and brush embroidery techniques to decorate the teacups. For the flower pattern, see the illustration (page 43).

13. Pipe dots of icing with a #2 tip along the top of the teacup and at the bottom edge of the teacup lip. Pipe the same dots around the edge of the saucer.

A

B

C

D

E

F

G

H

I

Cakes

Cakes

If you can imagine an object, you can probably make it into a cake. This chapter contains some of Confetti Cakes' most requested creations. Some of them are less challenging and others are extremely time consuming, but you can do it. Just follow the instructions and use the templates — and feel free to get creative with your colors and decorations.

When I am working on a particularly elaborate cake, I start several days or a week in advance so I have plenty of time to complete all the decorations and give them time to dry. Make sure you read the entire set of instructions before you begin any project so there are no surprises. The cake will seem less time consuming if you give yourself several days or a week to work on it, and plan one step per day: making the sugar decorations, preparing the base, baking the cakes and making fillings, assembling the cakes, and then decorating.

Also, be sure to pay careful attention to the structural elements of the cakes. You do not want to put a whole lot of effort into something only to have it fall apart! If you follow the advice in these instructions, that will not happen. The bigger and heavier your cakes, the more support they need. If you are making cakes even larger than we describe here, consider using extra layers of cardboard or foam core to support them — you might want to glue two or three pieces together to make them really solid.

Most of these projects also include instructions for making cake bases covered in fondant. If you want to save time, you can skip this step in some cases and just assemble your cake on the plate or platter on which you plan to present it.

For most of the projects in this chapter, you can use any of the cake and filling recipes in the Basic Recipes section of the book (pages 49–52). Occasionally we recommend flavors that work well; however, we always suggest a sturdy filling such as buttercream or ganache.

Bow Cake

YIELD: 8 TO 10 SERVINGS

This is a simple cake to make, and the result is stunning.
It is one of the first cakes I started making for clients,
and people still call to request it. The square shape is clean
and elegant, but the loops on top make it fun and colorful.
This can also be made as a large gift box cake by
substituting one large ribbon bow for the loops (see Mini
Present Cakes on page 136).

What You Need

CAKE

1 cake recipe
(see *Basic Recipes* pages 49–52)

1 frosting recipe
(see *Basic Recipes* pages 55–57)

½ recipe Royal Icing (page 58)

MATERIALS

2½ pounds gum paste

Food-coloring gels: lemon yellow, rose pink, bakers rose, sunset orange, electric green

Shortening (for rolling out gum paste)

2 tablespoons egg whites

6 pounds fondant (store-bought or page 60) (4 pounds if not making a cake base)

Cornstarch (for rolling out fondant)

Luster dusts: pearl, yellow

Lemon extract

EQUIPMENT

Parchment paper

Toothpicks

Plastic mat

Small rolling pin

Paring knife or X-acto knife

Ruler

Small paintbrush

Twenty-five 4-inch cloth-covered wires

Scissors

Large rolling pin

Strainer

Dry pastry brush

Fondant smoothers

One 10-inch square cake base (made from three pieces of foam core or store-bought)

One 6-inch square cardboard or foam core

Small serrated knife

Small offset spatula

1 large paintbrush

Pastry bag and coupler

#2 pastry tip

Decorative ribbon (for the cake base)

White glue (for the decorative ribbon)

TECHNIQUES

Dyeing fondant and gum paste (page 40)

Filling cake (page 31)

Crumb coating cake (page 33)

Covering cake with fondant (page 34)

Measuring gum paste and fondant (page 61)

Method

ONE WEEK AHEAD: MAKE THE DECORATIONS

1. Cover a flat surface with parchment paper for all the pieces to rest before assembly.

2. Divide the gum paste into four 7-ounce portions (each about the size of a tennis ball), and one 12-ounce portion. Dye the 7-ounce portions pale yellow, yellow, pale pink, and peach, respectively. Dye the 12-ounce section coral. Set aside 5 ounces of the coral for the balls around the bottom border.

3. On a plastic mat greased with shortening, roll each 7-ounce portion of colored gum paste into a sheet approximately ⅛ inch thick and cut into six 8½-inch by ¾-inch strips. You need approximately 22 bows, and should make a few extra in case of breakage.

4. Dip a brush in the egg white and coat the lower third of each strip. Place a cloth-covered wire on top of the egg white. The wire should extend about 1½ inches into the strip with the remaining 2½ inches hanging off the strip. Fold over the top of the strip and pinch the wire between the two ends of the gum paste. Shape the strip into a loop, and set it on its side on the parchment paper to dry.

5. On the greased mat, roll out the 5 ounces of coral gum paste into a long rope, approximately ⅜ inch thick. Use a paring knife to cut the rope at ⅜-inch intervals, until you have about 70 pieces. (Re-roll if needed until you have enough pieces.) Roll the pieces into round balls and place on the parchment paper to dry.

6. Dye 2 pounds of the fondant pale yellow. Roll out to about ⅛ inch thick and cover the cake base.

MAKE AND ASSEMBLE THE CAKE

1. Prepare the cake batter and bake in a half-sheet pan as directed in the recipe. Let it cool for 20 minutes, remove from pan, then wrap tightly in plastic wrap and freeze for at least one hour. (This makes the cake easier to cut.)

2. While the cakes are chilling, make the frosting and Royal Icing.

3. Cut the cake into three 6-inch squares. You will need to piece the middle 6-inch layer of the tier from leftover pieces of the cake.

4. Place a dab of filling on the 6-inch-square cake board and place a cake square on it. Top the cake with approximately ½ inch of filling, add the middle cake square, top that with ½ inch of filling, and place a third cake square on top. After the top layer is placed, push down slightly to secure the layers.

5. Even the sides by trimming any overhang with a serrated knife. If the cake shifts while you trim, chill the cake for at least an hour before cutting. Cut away any cardboard that is showing, either with a serrated knife or scissors.

6. Crumb coat the cake with a very thin layer of filling.

7. Dye the remaining fondant light green. On a surface dusted with cornstarch, roll out to ¼ inch thick and carefully cover the entire cake. Create a shimmer effect by painting the fondant with a mixture of pearl and yellow luster dusts mixed with lemon extract.

8. Place a dab of Royal Icing in the center of the cake base. Place the cake on the base and center it with your hands or fondant smoothers.

9. Attach the coral balls around the bottom edge of the cake, using tiny dabs of Royal Icing from a pastry bag fitted with a #2 tip as your glue.

10. Roll a ½-inch ball of gum paste (using any of the extra pink gum paste). Attach to the center of the top of the cake with a drop of water. Insert wire ends of the dried loop bows, one at a time, through the ball and into the center of the cake. If the wires are too long, snip them with scissors. Fill the entire ball with loop bows, starting with one loop bow pointing straight up in the very center and working around the center bow to the outside, creating a varied pattern with the colors.

11. Use white glue to attach a decorative ribbon around the cake base.

Baby Blocks Cake

YIELD: 15 TO 20 SERVINGS

This is the perfect cake to make for a baby shower or a baby's first birthday. Each block is made on its own cake board and is a separate cake. When we bring all the cakes together, they resemble an adorable set of blocks. You don't need to make any of the decorations ahead of time, but you may make the bear up to a week in advance. It is often easier to handle the sugar decorations when they have a day or two to dry, but it is not absolutely necessary. To save time, you can omit the bear — the blocks are cute on their own!

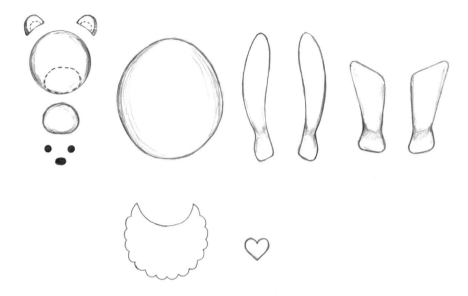

What You Need

CAKE

1 cake recipe (see *Basic Recipes* pages 49–52)

1 frosting recipe (see *Basic Recipes* pages 55–57)

½ recipe Royal Icing (page 58)

MATERIALS

4¾ pounds gum paste

Food-coloring gels: lemon yellow, bakers rose, willow green, violet, buckeye brown, royal blue

Shortening (for rolling out gum paste)

6½ pounds fondant (store-bought or page 60) or 4 pounds if not using a cake base

Cornstarch (for rolling out fondant)

EQUIPMENT

Toothpicks

Plastic mat

Small rolling pin

Paring knife or X-acto knife

Pastry tips: #804 (or a ⅜-inch round cutter), #802 (or a ¼-inch round cutter)

Optional: Bib cutter (or 1½-inch round fluted biscuit cutter and 1-inch round cutter for the bear's bib)

Small heart cutter (for bib)

Paintbrush

Large rolling pin

Strainer

Dry pastry brush

Fondant smoothers

One 16-inch round cake base (made from three pieces of foam core or store-bought)

Four 4 x 4-inch cardboard squares or foam core

Small serrated knife

Ruler

Small offset spatula

Scissors

Number and letter cutters, approximately 2 inches high

Stitching tool (optional)

Cutters (approximately 2 inches high) to decorate the sides of the blocks: heart, bear, star, onesie

3 wooden dowels, ¼ inch wide

#806 pastry tip (or a ½-inch round cutter for creating polka dots on cake base)

Decorative ribbon (for the cake base)

White glue (for the decorative ribbon)

TECHNIQUES

Dyeing fondant and gum paste (page 40)

Filling cake (page 31)

Crumb coating cake (page 33)

Covering cake with fondant (page 34)

Doweling cakes (page 37)

Measuring gum paste and fondant (page 61)

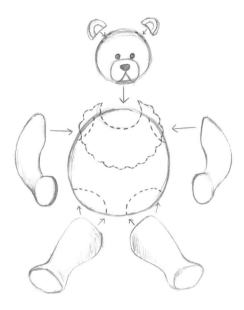

Method

MAKE THE DECORATIONS

Teddy Bear

1.   Dye 4 ounces of gum paste brown. Use about ½ ounce of white gum paste for the bib, a pinch of pink gum paste for the ears, a pinch of green gum paste for the heart on his bib, and a pinch of dark brown for the eyes and nose.

2.   On a plastic mat greased with shortening, roll a 2¼-inch-diameter ball for the bear's body and a 1¼-inch-diameter ball for the bear's head. Attach the bear's head on top of the body with a drop of water. (The larger ball will naturally slouch due to gravity — that's good, because you want the bear to be cuddly!)

3.   Roll out two cylinder shapes, 1½ inches x ½ inch, for the bear's legs. Pinch them at the ankles and squeeze the ends between your thumb and index finger to form the feet. Roll out two more cylinders, about 1¾ inches x ½ inch, for the bear's arms. Pinch them at the wrists and squeeze the ends to form the hands.

4.   Attach the legs to the bottom of the body with drops of water. Attach the arms to the sides of the body, curving them around so the hands lay on top of the legs.

5.   For the muzzle, roll a ball approximately ¾ inch wide and cut it in half. Use a toothpick to make indentations in an upside-down Y shape for the bear's mouth. Attach the muzzle to the lower half of the bear's face with a drop of water.

6.   For the ears, roll out a small marble of brown gum paste approximately ⅛ inch thick. Cut out a ⅜-inch circle using the back of a #804 pastry tip (or a ⅜-inch round cutter) and then cut it in half. Repeat the process with an even smaller marble of pink gum paste and an #802 tip (or a ¼-inch round cutter). Attach the smaller halves into the larger ears. Curve the ears slightly and attach them to the head of the bear with a drop of water.

7.   For the eyes and nose, use dark brown gum paste to form two tiny balls for the eyes and one slightly larger, oval-shaped ball for the nose. Attach them to the bear's face with tiny dabs of water.

8.   Roll out the white gum paste to ¹⁄₁₆ inch thick. Cut out the bib with a 1½-inch round fluted cutter. Use a 1-inch round cutter to cut a circle out of one side of the bib so it fits around the bear's neck. Finish the bear by rolling out a marble-sized piece of apple green gum paste to ¹⁄₁₆ inch thick. Cut out a ½-inch heart and attach to the center of the bib with a dab of water. Place the bib around the bear's neck and secure it with a drop of water. If the water is not holding the bear together, use pasteurized egg whites or Royal Icing as your glue.

Cake Base (Optional)

1.   Dye approximately 2½ pounds of fondant baby blue and roll out to about ⅛ inch thick. Cover the cake base with the fondant.

2.   If you want to decorate the base with polka dots, roll out 4 ounces (size of 2 golf balls) white fondant or gum paste to ¹⁄₁₆ inch thick on a plastic mat greased with shortening. Use the #806 pastry tip or a ½-inch round cutter to cut out about 35 dots. Using a paring knife or X-acto knife clean up the edges of the dots if necessary. Use tiny drops of water to stick them to the base in a random pattern.

3.   Set the base aside to dry for at least a few hours before stacking the cakes on top.

MAKE AND ASSEMBLE THE CAKE

1.   Prepare the cake batter and bake in 2 half-sheet pans as directed in the recipe. Let it cool for 20 minutes, remove from pan, then wrap tightly in plastic wrap and freeze for at least one hour. (This makes the cake easier to cut.)

2.   While the cake is chilling, make the frosting and Royal Icing.

3.   Cut the cake into twelve 4 x 4-inch squares.

4.   Spread a dab of filling on the square cake board and place a cake square on it. Top the cake with approximately ½ inch of filling, add the middle cake square, top that with ½ inch of filling, and place a third cake square on top. After the top layer is placed, push down slightly to secure the layers. Repeat for the other 3 blocks.

5.   Chill the cake for at least an hour before cutting. Even the sides by trimming any overhang with a serrated knife. Cut away any cardboard that is showing, either with a serrated knife or scissors. Crumb coat the cake with a very thin layer of filling.

6.   For each block roll out 1 pound of the fondant to ¼ inch thick. Cover the cakes with the fondant.

7.   Divide 4 pounds of gum paste into four 1-pound portions. Dye the portions pale green, pale blue, lilac, and pale yellow. On plastic mats greased with shortening, roll out one color at a time into sheets approximately ¹⁄₁₆ inch thick. For each sheet, use the ruler and paring knife to create 20 straight stripes, about ½ inch wide, for the edges of the blocks. All the stripes should be cut to fit on your blocks so sizing may vary. Make horizontal stripes the exact width of the cake layer, approximately 4¼ inches, and the vertical stripes to be approximately 3 inches. Reserve the remaining colored gum paste for the letters, numbers, and symbols to decorate the blocks. Cover it tightly in plastic wrap to keep it from drying out.

8.   Using a paintbrush slightly dampened with water, brush the edges of the cake sides and apply the stripes, one side at a time. If you want to apply stitching marks, use the stitching tool or the end of a toothpick to make the tiny indentations along the stripes of gum paste after the stripes are on the cakes.

9.   For each block roll out the remaining gum paste and cut out 2 of the same letter per block (for example, two A's) and 2 of the same symbol per block (for example, two hearts). Cut out one number (1, 2, 3, or 4) to be placed on top of each block. Attach all the decorations to the blocks with a water-dampened brush. Using a stitching tool, add stitching details, if desired.

10. Choose the one block that will be placed on top and set it aside. Attach the remaining three blocks in the center of the cake base with a dab of Royal Icing. Make sure one edge of each block is facing toward the center, and that you place the blocks close enough to one another (about an inch apart at the center corners) so that the fourth block can be placed on top.

11. Cut three wooden dowels to the height of the three bottom cakes. Insert a dowel straight down into the inside corner of each block, forming a triangular pattern with the dowels, staying at least ¾ inch from the edge so the dowel doesn't go through the side of the cake. Make sure that the cake placed on top will cover the three dowels.

12. Spread ½ tablespoon of Royal Icing over each of the dowels. Place and center the remaining block on top. Attach the teddy bear on top of the cake with a few dabs of Royal Icing.

13. Use white glue to attach a decorative ribbon around the cake base.

HOT TIP

■ To save the amount of cake you use, you may want to piece cake together to achieve a 4-inch square. Use the pieces as your middle layer in the block.

Baseball Hat Cake

YIELD: 10 TO 15 SERVINGS

I love this cake because it looks just like a real hat and you can customize it with your favorite team, logo, initial, or symbol. The stitching details make it especially realistic. Sometimes we cover the cake base with brown sugar to make it look like the dirt of a baseball field, or use green Royal Icing as blades of grass.

What You Need

CAKE

2 cake recipes (see *Basic Recipes* pages 49–52)

2 filling recipes (see *Basic Recipes* pages 55–57)

MATERIALS

12 ounces gum paste

Food-coloring gels: lemon yellow, leaf green, navy blue

Shortening (for rolling out gum paste)

3½ pounds fondant (store-bought or page 60)

Cornstarch (for rolling out fondant)

EQUIPMENT

1 piece lightweight cardboard, oak tag, or the flap of a bakery box, at least 8 x 6 inches

Paring knife or X-acto knife

Empty paper towel roll

Toothpicks

Plastic mat

Small rolling pin

Ruler

Stitching tool (optional)

Large rolling pin

Strainer

Dry pastry brush

Fondant smoothers

One 14-inch round cake base (made from three pieces of foam core or store-bought)

Small serrated knife

Small offset spatula

One 9-inch round cardboard or foam core

Pastry tips: #3, #802 (or a ¼-inch round circle cutter)

Star cutter, approximately 3 inches high (optional)

Paintbrush

Dish of water

Scissors

Decorative ribbon

White glue

TECHNIQUES

Dyeing fondant and gum paste (page 40)

Covering cake base with fondant (page 36)

Splitting cake (page 29)

Filling cake (page 31)

Sculpting cake (page 32)

Crumb coating cake (page 33)

Covering cake with fondant (page 34)

Measuring gum paste and fondant (page 61)

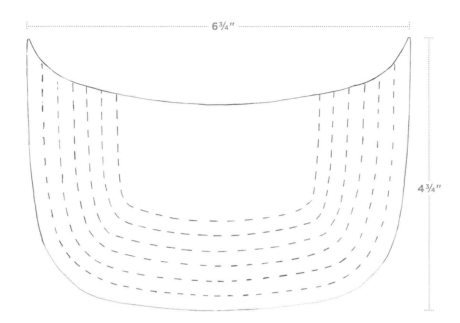

6¾"

4¾"

Method

1.   Cut the shape of a hat brim out of the lightweight cardboard. (See template, above.) Shape the cardboard into a curved form by folding it in half and then placing it on top of something round like an empty paper towel roll.

2.   Dye 10 ounces of gum paste navy blue. On a plastic mat greased with shortening, roll out 8 ounces of it to ⅛ inch thick and large enough to fit over the brim. Trim away the excess gum paste where the brim will join the hat.

3.   Cover the pre-cut board for the hat brim with the gum paste and, using the stitching tool, make 6 lines that are ¼ inch apart along the edge of the brim. Put back on the paper towel roll and let it dry for at least 2 days.

4.   Roll out the green fondant to ⅛ inch thick and cover the cake base.

MAKE AND ASSEMBLE THE CAKE

1.   Prepare the cake batter as directed in the recipe. Fill three 9-inch round pans ¾ full and bake for 1 hour. Let it cool for 20 minutes, remove from pans, then wrap tightly in plastic wrap and freeze for at least one hour. (This makes the cake easier to cut.)

2.   While the cake is chilling, make the frosting.

3.   Prepare three 9-inch round layers, each 1 inch high, splitting a thicker layer if necessary.

4.   Place a dab of filling on the round cake board and place the first round layer of cake on it. Top the cake with ½ inch of filling, add another layer of cake, top that layer with ½ inch of filling, and top with the remaining round. After the top layer of cake is on, push down slightly to secure the layers. Place the cake in the freezer and chill for 1 hour.

5.   Using a serrated knife, sculpt the cake so it looks like an upside-down

bowl, trimming a little at a time. For extra detail, carve away a hole, approximately 2¼ inches wide, 1½ inches high, and 2 inches deep, in the back for the adjustable strap. Cut away any cardboard that is showing, either with a serrated knife or scissors.

6.   To add dimension and to make the hat look like fabric, cut away a few slivers near the top of the hat. When covered in fondant, these divots will look like dents in the fabric. The carved cake should be approximately 7¼ inches front to back and 3¾ inches tall. Crumb coat the cake with a very thin layer of filling.

7.   Dye 1½ pounds of fondant navy blue (be sure it matches the gum paste). On a surface lightly dusted with cornstarch, roll to ¼ inch thick and place it on the cake. Make sure to apply fondant to the backside of the hat where the head strap will go and to trim the bottom edge carefully. Press the fondant into the divots you created to give it a realistic shape.

HOT TIPS

■ Depending on your cake pans, you can bake three separate 9-inch cakes that are 1 inch high or two 8-inch round cakes, at least 2 inches high (one cake recipe). The thicker cakes will take longer to bake.

■ If you have trouble with the brim of the hat, or your gum paste does not have time to dry, leave the gum paste attached to the cardboard and attach it to the cake. Just remember not to eat the cardboard.

8. Attach the cake to the base with a dab of Royal Icing. (Remember to leave enough room for the brim of the hat.)

9. Using a paring knife or scalpel, divide the hat into 8 equal sections. **Be careful just to score the lines, not cut all the way through.** First make a line going from the front to the back, then one from side to side. Next make two diagonal lines that crisscross in the middle. On both sides of each line, create stitching marks using a toothpick or a stitching tool.

10. To make the rivets, take the tip of the #802 pastry tip and create holes about 2 inches from the top of the hat in each of the eight sections. Use the tip of a #3 tip to create a smaller hole inside the first hole to make it look like a rivet.

11. Roll a marble-sized ball of navy gum paste and flatten it to create a button for the top of the hat. Using a dab of water attach it to the hat where all the lines intersect.

12. On the greased mat, roll out the remaining navy gum paste to 1/16 inch thick, to form the head strap. Cut a strip at least 4½ inches long and ¾ inch wide. Divide the strip into two pieces, 2 inches long and 2½ inches long. Round the end of the 2-inch piece and place the rounded end on top of the other piece, attaching it with a dab of water. Using the #802 and #3 tips as in step 10, make a few rivets on each side of the strap. With a drop of water, attach the ends of the strap to the inside of the hole you made on the backside of the hat. Use the stitching tool to go along the outside of the hole. This is a great place to personalize the hat: you can write a name or favorite number on top of the opening with Royal Icing or letters and numbers cut out of gum paste.

13. Roll any extra navy fondant you have into a ball and place it in the center front of the hat on the cake base. This will act as a support when you attach the brim.

14. Carefully release the gum-paste brim from the cardboard. Attach it to the hat with a few drops of water, pressing the brim gently into the hat. Create a stitched line where the brim meets the hat to make it look like a proper seam.

15. For the star symbol pictured here, dye a small amount of fondant or gum paste yellow, roll out to 1/16 inch thick, and use a cutter to cut out a star. Attach it to the hat with a small amount of water. Create stitch marks around the edge of the star so it looks as though it was sewn onto the hat.

16. Use white glue to attach a decorative ribbon around the cake base.

Chinese Takeout Box Cake

YIELD: 8 TO 10 SERVINGS

When a client called and requested this cake, I just couldn't wait to make it!
This is perfect for a Chinese food lover or for a party with an Asian theme.
You could even make this as a special surprise dessert to accompany a takeout
dinner on an ordinary Sunday night. The fortune cookies are made out of sugar
and you can write your own special message if you want. If you are short on
time use actual fortune cookies to accompany the cake.

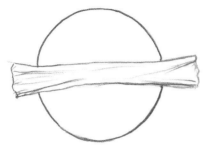

What You Need

CAKE

1 cake recipe
(see *Basic Recipes* pages 49–52)

1 frosting recipe
(see *Basic Recipes* pages 55–57)

½ recipe Royal Icing (page 58)

MATERIALS

1 pound gum paste

Food-coloring gels: super red,
egg yellow, buckeye brown

Shortening (for rolling out
gum paste)

4 pounds fondant (store-
bought or page 60)

Cornstarch (for rolling out
fondant)

Vodka

Metallic silver luster dust

Lemon extract

EQUIPMENT

Toothpicks

Plastic mat

Small rolling pin

3-inch round cookie cutter

Paper towels

Ruler

Paring knife or X-acto knife

Food marker

Pastry bag and coupler

#2 pastry tip

One 4-inch by 3½-inch
foam core board

Small serrated knife

Small offset spatula

Large rolling pin

Strainer

Dry pastry brush

Fondant smoothers

Small paintbrush

Small dish of water

Scissors

One 15-inch-long
cloth-covered wire

TECHNIQUES

Dyeing fondant and gum
paste (page 40)

Splitting cake (page 29)

Filling cake (page 31)

Sculpting cake (page 32)

Crumb coating cake
(page 33)

Covering cake with
fondant (page 34)

Piecing fondant (page 36)

Measuring gum paste
and fondant (page 61)

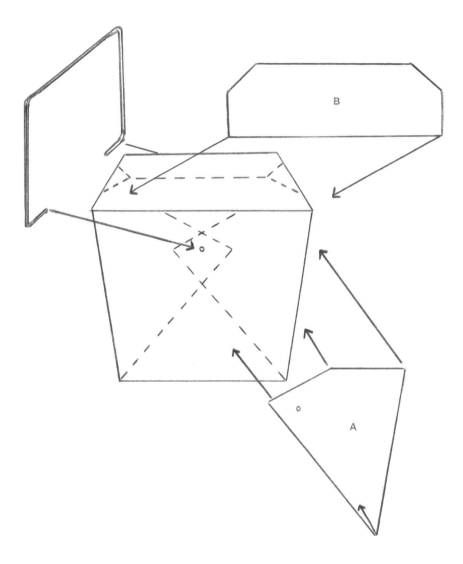

Method

AT LEAST 2 DAYS IN ADVANCE: MAKE THE
FORTUNE COOKIES

1. Dye 2 ounces of gum paste caramel color.

2. On a plastic mat greased with shortening, roll out the gum
paste to $^1/_{16}$ inch thick. Use the 3-inch round cutter to cut out
3 circles. Roll 3 paper towels into ropes, approximately 4
inches long and ¼ inch thick.

3. Place a paper towel in the middle of each circle and fold
the gum paste as shown in the illustration opposite. Let the
cookies dry on a tray for at least 2 days.

4. Before assembling, make the Royal Icing.

5. For the fortunes, roll out approximately 1 ounce of white
gum paste to $^1/_{16}$ inch thick and cut three strips, ½ inch wide
and 2 inches long.

6. Keep one end flat and curve the other end to form an arc.
Let the fortunes dry overnight. Once the fortunes are dry,
write your fortune on it with a food marker. Attach the flat end
inside the fortune cookie with a small amount of Royal Icing.

ONE DAY IN ADVANCE: MAKE AND ASSEMBLE THE CAKE

1. Prepare the cake batter and bake in a half-sheet pan as
directed in the recipe. Let it cool for 20 minutes, remove from
pan, then wrap tightly in plastic wrap and freeze for at least
one hour. (This makes the cake easier to cut.)

2. While the cake is chilling, make the frosting.

3. Cut four 5 x 5-inch squares out of the cake.

4. Place a dab of filling on the 4 x 3½-inch cake board and
place the first square of cake on it. Top the bottom layer with
approximately ½ inch of filling, and add the next three
squares of cake, alternating with ½ inch of filling. You will
have 4 layers of cake and 3 layers of filling. Push down slightly
on the block to secure the layers. Place in the freezer and chill
for 1 hour.

5. Using a serrated knife, carve the block to a 5 x 4-inch
rectangle on top that tapers to about a 4 x 3½-inch rectangle
on the bottom. Cut away any cardboard that is showing either
with a serrated knife or scissors. Crumb coat the cake with a
very thin layer of filling.

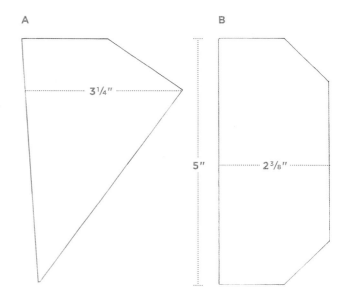

A   B

3¼" 5" 2³/₈"

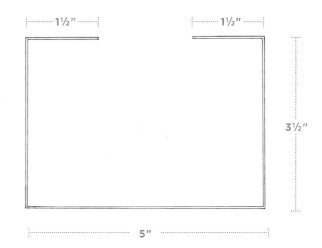

1½" 1½" 3½" 5"

6. On a plastic mat greased with shortening, roll out 4 pounds of fondant to approximately ¼ inch thick. Cut the fondant into five pieces, 4 for the sides and 1 top piece. Cut the pieces slightly larger than the dimensions of the cake to make it easier to assemble.

7. On the greased mat, roll out 8 ounces of gum paste to ¹⁄₁₆ inch thick. Cut out two triangular flaps using **template A,** turn it over, and cut out two more flaps (they will be pointing in the opposite direction). Repeat the process with **template B.**

8. Starting with the triangular flaps cut from **template A,** moisten the backs with water and line up the longest side of the flaps with the longest outside edge of the cake. The flaps should overlap at the center of the box. Repeat on the opposite side.

9. To apply the top flaps, again line up the longest sides of the flaps (cut using **template B**) with the longer edge of the cake and attach them to the top of the cake. Where the flaps meet in the center, cut a 1-inch slit and insert the top flap into the lower flap.

10. To form the cloth-covered wire into a handle, start at one end of the wire, bend it using the measurements on the template opposite. Use the silver luster dust mixed with 1 teaspoon of lemon extract to paint the wire silver. Set aside to dry.

12. Once the cake is finished let it sit overnight before you paint it. This allows the fondant to harden slightly. Using a paint mixture of red food-coloring gel and vodka, paint the words **ENJOY** and **THANK YOU** and illustrate the pagoda (see template). Of course, you can add any other saying or symbols you wish. To transfer the pagoda design directly onto the cake, make a photocopy of the template, trace the design with a pencil, turn the pencil side onto the cake, and rub the back of the paper gently with a pencil. The rubbing will come off onto the cake and you will be able paint over the lines.

13. Using a toothpick, poke a hole in the sides of the box, ½ inch from the top, for the wire handle. Insert the handle into the holes. If it does not stay on its own, glue it in with dabs of white Royal Icing.

Two-Tiered Cake

YIELD: 30 TO 35 SERVINGS

Here is a two-tiered square cake that applies the fundamentals of doweling and tiering a cake. Think of it as a blank canvas — and you are the artist. The HAPPY BIRTHDAY version is my favorite to make for anyone's big day. We also provide four other variations. Pick one of these five design techniques on the following pages and follow the instructions exactly, or make it your very own, personalizing it with specific colors.

What You Need

CAKE

2 cake recipes
(see *Basic Recipes* pages 49–52)

2 frosting recipes
(see *Basic Recipes* page 55–57)

1 recipe Royal Icing (page 58)

MATERIALS

2 pounds gum paste

Food-coloring gels: lemon yellow, bakers rose, leaf green, violet, super red, sunset orange, royal blue

Shortening (for rolling out gum paste)

5¼ pounds fondant (store-bought or page 60)

Cornstarch (for rolling out fondant)

EQUIPMENT

Toothpicks

Plastic mat

Small rolling pin

Extra pastry tips: for polka dots: #802 (¼ inch), #804 (⅜ inch), #806 (½ inch), #808 (⅝ inch) and round cutters: ⅞ inch, 1¼ inch, 1½ inch

Letter cutters (for HAPPY BIRTHDAY), approximately 1¼ inches high

Large rolling pin

Strainer

Dry pastry brush

Fondant smoothers

One 12-inch square cake base (made from three pieces of foam core or store-bought)

Ruler

Paring knife or X-acto knife

One 5-inch square cardboard or foam core

One 8-inch square cardboard or foam core

Small serrated knife

Small offset spatula

4 dowels

Paintbrush

Dish of water

Pastry bag and coupler

#2 pastry tip

Scissors

Decorative ribbon

White glue

TECHNIQUES

Dyeing fondant and gum paste (page 40)

Covering cake base with fondant (page 36)

Filling cake (page 31)

Crumb coating cake (page 33)

Covering cake with fondant (page 34)

Doweling cakes (page 37)

Dyeing Royal Icing (page 40)

Filling a pastry bag (page 38)

Piping dots (page 39)

Measuring gum paste and fondant (page 61)

Method

AT LEAST ONE DAY IN ADVANCE: MAKE THE DECORATIONS

1. **For the letters and dots:** dye approximately 8 ounces of gum paste purple for the letters and the remaining 1½ pounds into 10 to 12 different colors for the dots. You need approximately 120 dots to cover the cake, or 10–12 different-sized dots of each color. If you are short on time it is not essential for the dots to dry, but they are easier to handle once they have had a few hours to harden.

2. On a plastic mat greased with shortening, roll out the purple gum paste to approximately ¼ inch thick. Cut out **HAPPY BIRTHDAY.** Use a paring knife or X-acto knife to clean up the edges of the letters. Let the letters dry flat for at least a few hours.

3. On a plastic mat greased with shortening, roll out one color of gum paste at a time to approximately 1/16 inch thick. Use the various sizes of pastry tips and round cutters to cut out about 10 different-sized dots of each color. Using a paring knife, clean up the edges of the dots. Let them dry flat for at least a few hours.

For the cake base: Dye approximately 5¼ pounds of fondant pale yellow. Roll out 2 pounds to ⅛ inch thick and cover the cake base. Wrap the remaining fondant in plastic wrap.

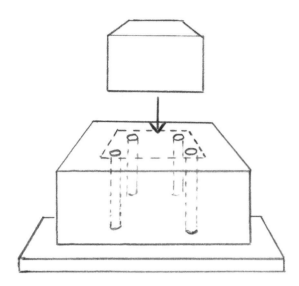

MAKE AND ASSEMBLE THE CAKE

1. Prepare the cake batter and bake in 2 half-sheet pans as directed in the recipe. Let it cool for 20 minutes, remove from pans, then wrap tightly in plastic wrap and freeze for at least one hour. (This makes the cake easier to cut.)

2. While the cakes are chilling, make the frosting and Royal Icing.

3. Cut 6 layers of cake: three 5-inch squares and three 8-inch squares. You will have to piece cake together to get one of your 8-inch squares. Use this as the middle layer of the tier.

4. Build one tier at a time — you are making one tier from the 5-inch squares and the other from the 8-inch squares. Place a dab of filling on the appropriately sized cake board and attach the first layer of cake. Top the cake with ½ inch of filling, add the middle cake square, top that with ½ inch of filling, and place the third cake square on top. When the top layer of cake is on, push down slightly to secure the layers.

5. Freeze the cake for 1 hour. Make sure the tiers are completely square by trimming any overhanging cake with a serrated knife. Cut away any cardboard that is showing with a serrated knife or scissors.

6. Crumb coat the tiers with a very thin layer of filling.

7. On a surface dusted with cornstarch, roll out the remaining yellow fondant to ¼ inch thick. Cover each tier with fondant. You need approximately 1¼ pounds to cover the 5-inch square tier and 2 pounds to cover the 8-inch square tier. Trim the edges carefully so they look straight and clean.

8. Use Royal Icing to glue the 8-inch tier to the cake base. Center the cake on the base with your hands or fondant smoothers.

9. Cut 4 dowels to the height of your cake and insert them straight down into the cake, following the diagram above.

10. Spread 2 tablespoons of icing over the area within the dowels. Place the 5-inch tier on top and center it.

11. Dye a small amount of icing light green and, using a #2 tip, pipe a border of dots, spaced about ⅛ inch apart, around the base of both tiers.

12. Use white glue to attach a decorative ribbon around the cake base.

13. Use icing to glue the letters to one side of the cake. When the letters are attached (and not sliding) pipe a line of green dots on each letter (see photo).

14. Attach all the different-colored dots in a random pattern all over the cake base and tiers. Use dabs of water to attach the dots if they haven't dried and use dabs of icing if they have dried.

Stripes

With its bold, stylish pattern that reminds me of a designer fabric, this is a gorgeous cake for a chic, contemporary party.

What You Need

MATERIALS

1½ pounds gum paste

Food-coloring gels: electric pink, super red, buckeye brown, sunset orange, electric green

2 heart cookie cutters: 3-inch by 2¾-inch; 3¼-inch by 3-inch or cut by hand

Method

1. Follow steps 1 through 12 on page 183.

2. Divide the gum paste evenly into five sections and color the sections pink, red, brown, orange, and green.

3. On a plastic mat greased with shortening, roll out about 4 ounces of each gum-paste color to approximately $1/16$ inch thick. Use a ruler and a paring knife to create stripes of varying widths as follows: orange and green: ¼ inch wide; pink: $3/8$ inch wide; red and brown: $1/8$ inch wide. All the stripes should be cut to the exact height of the cake layers, approximately 4 inches. On the cake pictured here there are about 22 stripes of each color. Keep the gum paste covered in plastic when you are not using it.

4. Using a paintbrush dampened with water, brush a small section of the cake and begin to apply the stripes, one at a time, in a regular pattern. Space the stripes at roughly ¼-inch intervals.

5. Roll out approximately 1 ounce each of the red and pink gum paste to $1/16$ inch thick. Using heart cookie cutters, cut out a large heart from the red and a slightly smaller heart from the pink. Attach the pink heart to the center of the red heart with a drop of water. Then attach the layered heart in the center of the top tier with a drop of water. Do not use too much water, because red gum paste tends to bleed.

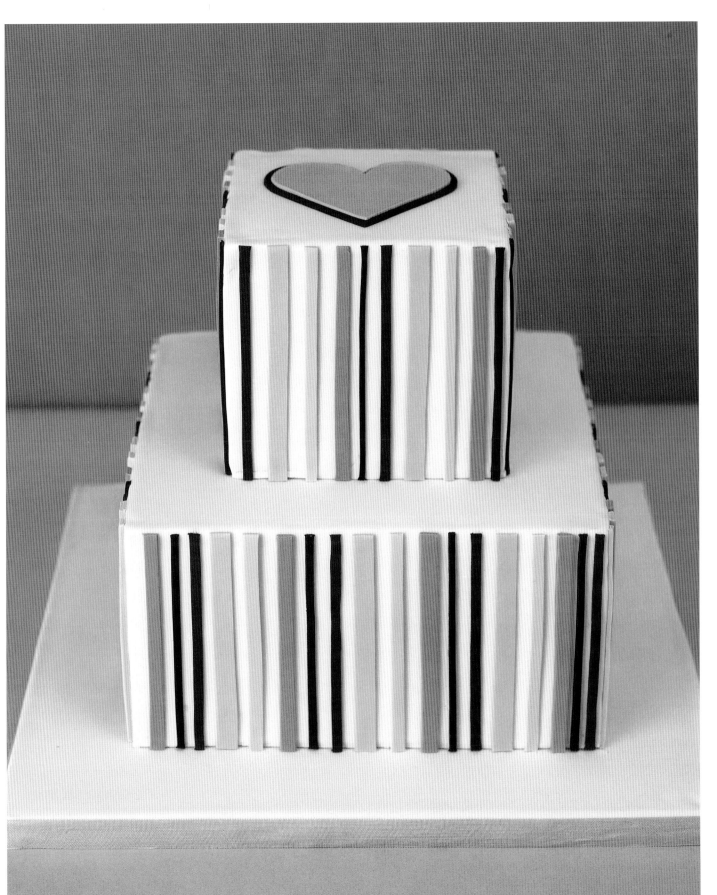

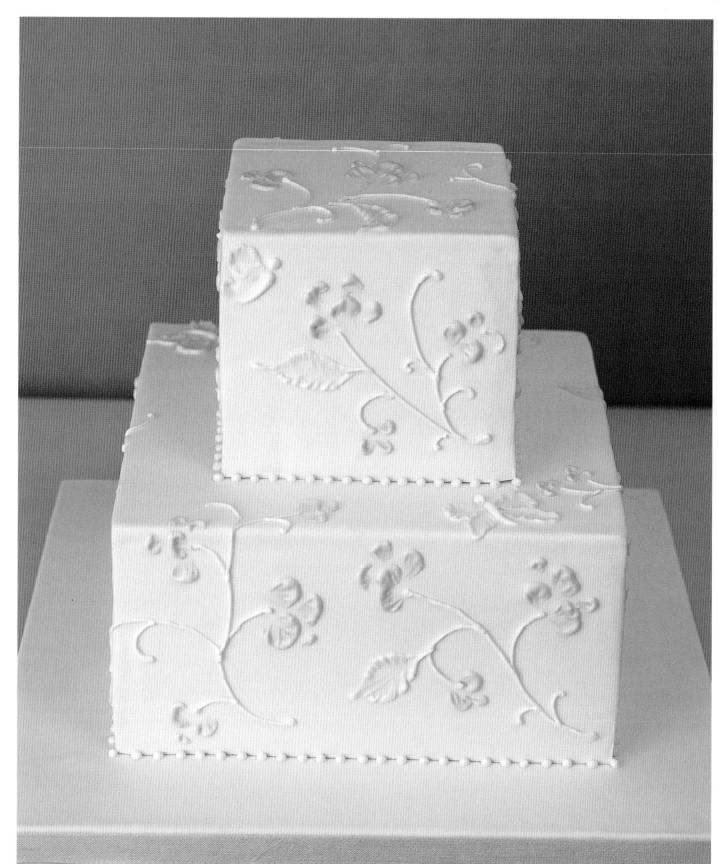

Brush Embroidery

What You Need

MATERIALS

½ recipe Royal Icing
(page 58)

Food-coloring gels: bakers
rose and willow green

EQUIPMENT

Pastry bag and coupler

Pastry tips: #2, #3

Paintbrushes

Small dish of pasteurized
egg whites

TECHNIQUES

Brush embroidery (page
43)

Method

1.   Follow steps 1 through 12 on page 183.

2.   Use the brush embroidery technique
(page 43) to create a pattern of flowers and
butterflies in pale pink and pale green all
over the cake.

HOT TIP

■ To add extra dimension
you can paint or dust the
flowers and butterflies once
the Royal Icing has dried.
Wait about 1 hour.

Hydrangeas

This cake uses floral relief, a wonderful technique that allows you to create a three-dimensional flower design without using wire. The end result is flowers that spring to life off the surface of the cake.

What You Need

MATERIALS

28 ounces gum paste

Leaf green food-coloring gel

1 recipe Royal Icing

Small dish of water

EQUIPMENT

Plastic mat

Small rolling pin

Shortening

Flower cutters: ½-inch
5-blossom

Leaf cutters: 1-inch,
1½-inch, and 2-inch

Egg carton

Paring knife or X-acto knife

Small paintbrush

Pastry bag

#2 pastry tip

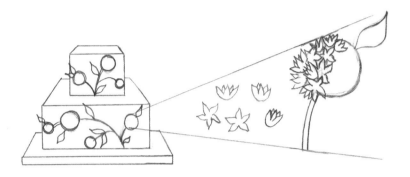

Method

1. Follow steps 1 through 12 on page 183.

2. On a greased plastic mat, roll out 12 ounces of gum paste to ¹⁄₁₆ inch thick. Use the flower cutter to cut out approximately 270 small flowers. Let them dry for a few hours in all different shapes on various planes of an egg carton.

3. Roll three 1-inch diameter balls, eight ¾-inch diameter balls, and eight ½-inch diameter balls of white gum paste and attach them to the cake with dabs of water.

4. Dye 16 ounces of gum paste leaf green and roll it out to approximately ¼ inch thick. Cut about 10 stems, approximately ¼ inch wide and of varying lengths ranging from 4 to 7 inches. Grease your fingers with shortening and round the straight edges of the stems. Apply the stems to the cake with dabs of water, as if they were connected to the balls of gum paste.

5. Use a small amount of Royal Icing to attach blossoms to the balls of gum paste on the cake, layering the blossoms to cover the entire ball. You should not be able to see any space between the blossoms.

6. Roll the leftover green gum paste to approximately ¹⁄₁₆ inch thick and cut out about 50 leaves in all different sizes, ranging from 1 to 2 inches long. Pinch one end to give it a stem and slightly point the other end to make it look like the top of a leaf. Attach the leaves to the stems with dabs of water and at the bases of the floral bunches.

7. Using a #2 tip, pipe a dot of icing to the center of each blossom.

HOT TIPS

▪ These flowers don't have to be white. Use the same color gum paste for the balls as you plan to use for the blossoms.

▪ If you are dusting the blossoms another color, do that before attaching them to the cake.

▪ If you want to use floral relief for a different kind of flower, before starting the project, find a design or pattern that you would like to replicate.

▪ The gum paste can sit awhile to become a little dryer, which makes it easier to handle.

Appliquéd Flowers

This is a modern take on a floral design that's so much fun to look at. It involves the appliqué technique, which allows you to create bold designs with flowers and other organic elements. To save time, you can simplify it by using fewer colors.

Method

1. Follow steps 1 through 12 on page 183.

2. Divide the gum paste evenly into seven portions and color the sections light pink, pink, red, chocolate brown, light blue, and orange. Keep one portion white.

3. On a plastic mat greased with shortening roll out each gum-paste color to $\frac{1}{16}$ inch thick. Use the different-sized cutters to cut out flowers in each color, about 10 per color.

4. Use a paintbrush dampened with water to stick the flowers onto the cake in a random pattern. Layer the flowers with different-sized and -colored flowers.

5. Make the Royal Icing. Divide into 3 sections, dye 1 pink and 1 light blue, keep 1 white. Embellish the flowers with light dots piped in the centers and around the edges, if desired.

Chocolate Embroidery
Wedding Cake

YIELD: 75 TO 80 SERVINGS

The first time I made this was for a *New York* magazine photo shoot. Then it was the winning cake on NBC's *Today Show Throws a Wedding*. But perhaps it is most famous for being Charlotte's wedding cake when she married Harry on HBO's *Sex and the City*. We have done this design so many times in so many different shapes, sizes, and color combinations, and I never get sick of it. Making this cake is a great way to improve your piping skills.

What You Need

CAKE

4 cake recipes (see *Basic Recipes* pages 49–52) to make three 4-inch rounds, ¾ inch high; three 6-inch rounds, 1 inch high; three 9-inch rounds, 1 inch high; three 12-inch rounds, ¾ inch high

3 frosting recipes (see *Basic Recipes* pages 55–57)

1 recipe Royal Icing (page 58)

MATERIALS

1½ pounds chocolate fondant

Shortening

9 pounds white fondant (store-bought or page 60)

Cornstarch (for rolling out fondant)

Food-coloring gels: rose pink, buckeye brown

EQUIPMENT

Plastic mat

Small rolling pin

Leaf cutters (optional)

Paring knife or X-acto knife

Egg carton

Toothpicks

One 14-inch round cake base (made from wood or store-bought)

Large rolling pin

Strainer

Dry pastry brush

Fondant smoothers

Ruler

Small serrated knife

Small offset spatula

4-inch, 6-inch, 9-inch, and 12-inch round cake boards

13 plastic dowels

Pastry bag and coupler

#2 pastry tip

Scissors

Decorative ribbon

White glue

TECHNIQUES

Dyeing fondant and gum paste (page 40)

Covering cake base with fondant (page 36)

Splitting cake (page 29)

Filling cake (page 31)

Crumb coating cake (page 33)

Doweling cakes (page 37)

Dyeing Royal Icing (page 40)

Filling a pastry bag (page 38)

Piping dots (page 39)

Method

MAKE THE DECORATIONS

Leaves

The leaves of this cake are made from chocolate fondant. You can make them ahead of time, so they are easier to apply, but that is not essential. If you make the leaves at least 2 days ahead and they have hardened, attach them to the cake with Royal Icing. If you make them the same day that you are decorating the cake, you will have to attach them with water.

1. On a plastic mat greased with shortening, roll out the chocolate fondant to approximately $1/16$ inch thick. Using leaf cutters (or paring knife or X-acto knife), cut out approximately 120 leaves. It's always a good idea to make a few extras in case of breakage. They look best when there is an assortment of sizes ranging from very tiny to larger leaves, thick and thin. Once they are all cut, pinch the sides to give them some dimension and a slight point at the tip, then place them in an egg carton to dry. This will encourage them to dry in curved shapes.

For the cake base: Dye all of the fondant pale pink. Roll out approximately 2 pounds to $1/8$ inch thick and cover the cake base. Wrap the remaining fondant with plastic.

HOT TIP

■ If you do not have chocolate fondant you can use either white fondant or gum paste and dye it brown. We use the chocolate fondant because it tastes great and has a rich color.

MAKE AND ASSEMBLE THE CAKE

1. Prepare the cake batter, pour into the pans specified, and bake according to the recipe. Let it cool for 20 minutes, remove from pans, then wrap tightly in plastic wrap and freeze for at least one hour. (This makes the cake easier to cut.)

2. While the cakes are chilling, make the frosting and Royal Icing.

3. Split cake layers if necessary to get the heights you need. For the 4-inch tier and the 12-inch tier (both 3 inches high), you need ¾-inch layers. For the 6-inch tier and the 9-inch tier (both 4 inches high), you'll need 1-inch layers.

4. Create the tiers one at a time on their cake rounds. Stack, fill (with ½-inch layers of filling), and crumb coat each tier. Each tier should have 3 layers of cake and 2 layers of filling. When the top layer is on, press gently to secure the layers.

5. Roll out the fondant to ¼ inch thick and cover each tier in pale pink fondant. See the fondant chart on page 61 to determine how much you'll need for each tier. Make sure that you pay careful attention to the edges. They should be completely straight and clean.

6. Use Royal Icing to glue the 12-inch tier in the center of the base. Let it set for a few minutes.

7. Cut and insert seven plastic dowels into the 12-inch tier. Put one in the center and six to form a circle around the center dowel. Stay within an 8-inch radius so you will not see the dowels once the 9-inch tier is placed on top. Attach the 9-inch tier on top of the 12-inch tier with icing. Continue in this manner, doweling this tier with five dowels and the 6-inch tier with one dowel, ending with the 4-inch tier on top.

8. Once the cake is completely tiered, pipe a border of brown icing dots around the bottom edge of each tier and one border of dots around the top of the 4-inch tier.

9. Pipe the embroidery design all over the cake in brown icing with a #2 tip, applying the leaves as you go. You can pipe it freehand, using the photograph and template as a guide. Or you can photocopy the template below. To transfer the design directly onto the cake, make a photocopy of the template, trace the design with pencil, turn the pencil side onto the cake and rub the back of the paper gently with a pencil. The rubbing will come off onto the cake and you will be able to follow the design.

10. Use white glue to attach a decorative ribbon around the cake base.

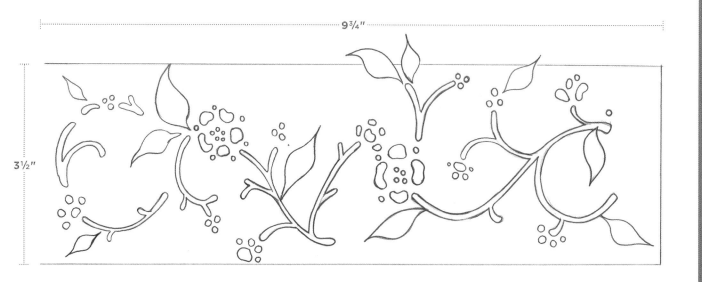

9¾"

3½"

Handbag Cake

YIELD: 25 TO 30 SERVINGS

Any fashionista will adore this bag. It makes an unforgettable Mother's Day or birthday gift. By changing the shape and adjusting the handle, you could make a briefcase-style bag, too. If you can make this cake, you will have the fundamentals to make any sculpted cake. Plan to make several of the elements ahead of time, and — even though this does not look like a tiered cake — you will need to dowel one tier inside the bag.

    This cake is all about the sugar decorations. It is the handle, bow, flowers, and pearls — all made from gum paste — that make this cake unique. Do not substitute fondant for gum paste here. You need the gum paste for structural reasons and to ensure that the details will dry and not crack.

What You Need

CAKE

3 cake recipes
(see *Basic Recipes* pages 49–52)

2 frosting recipes
(see *Basic Recipes* pages 55–57)

½ recipe Royal Icing (page 58)

MATERIALS

2 pounds gum paste

Food-coloring gels: lemon
yellow, rose pink, super red,
buckeye brown

Shortening (for rolling out
gum paste)

Luster dusts: metallic gold,
pearl

2 pounds white fondant
(store-bought or page 60)

5 pounds chocolate fondant

Cornstarch (for rolling out
fondant)

Lemon extract

EQUIPMENT

Toothpicks

Plastic mat

Small rolling pin

Ruler

Paring knife or X-acto knife

Stitching tool (optional)

Small paintbrush

Small dish of water

5-petal flower cutter set
(five different sizes)

Egg carton

1 cloth-covered wire

One 14-inch square cake
base (made from three pieces
of foam core or store-bought)

Large rolling pin

Strainer

Dry pastry brush

Fondant smoothers

Small serrated knife

Small offset spatula

One 9-inch by 4-inch
foam core board

One 7-inch by 3-inch
foam core board

Scissors

3 plastic dowels

Pastry bag and coupler

Pastry tips: #2, #4

Decorative ribbon

White glue

TECHNIQUES

Dyeing fondant and
gum paste (page 40)

Sugar bows and ribbons
(page 44)

Covering cake base in
fondant (page 36)

Filling cake (page 31)

Doweling sculpted cakes
(page 37)

Sculpting cake (page 32)

Crumb coating cake (page 33)

Covering cake in fondant
(page 34)

Piping dots (page 39)

Deconstructing sculpted
cakes (page 38)

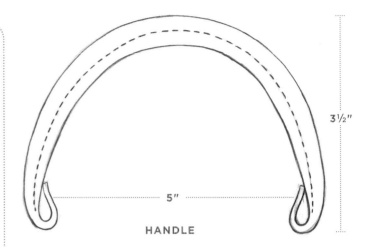

HANDLE

3½"

5"

Method

TWO DAYS TO 1 WEEK IN ADVANCE: MAKE THE DECORATIONS

Handle

1.   Dye 1 pound of gum paste caramel, using yellow, red, and brown food gels.

2.   On a plastic mat greased with shortening, roll out 8 ounces of gum paste to ½ inch thick. Cut a 12 x ¾-inch strip. Using a rolling pin, thin 1¾ inches on each end of the handle to ⅛ inch thick.

3.   With a stitching tool or toothpick, make stitch marks along the sides of the handle.

4.   Turn the handle on its side and curve it into a semicircle, approximately 4 inches wide. Fold the two thinned ends to form loops, approximately ¼ inch in diameter.

5.   To make the rings for the handle, roll out four 1-inch-long, ¼-inch-thick logs of white gum paste. Bend them into little L shapes. When they are dry, paint them with gold metallic luster dust.

Bow

1.   Using about 3 ounces the same caramel color as the handle, form a bow that is approximately 3 inches long.

2.   Use the stitching tool or a toothpick to make stitch marks in the gum paste before forming the bow. Reserve any extra caramel color gum paste for more leather detailing on the cake.

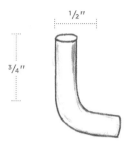

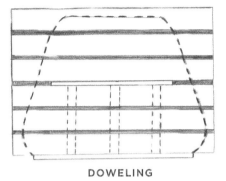

HANDLE RING

DOWELING

Flowers

1.   Dye approximately 2 ounces of gum paste pale pink. On a plastic mat greased with shortening, roll out the gum paste to $\frac{1}{16}$ inch thick.

2.   Cut out at least 8 flowers in various sizes using the 5-petal cutters. Let the flowers dry in different dimensions in an egg carton — they should not dry flat.

Pearls

1.   With your hands, roll out approximately 8 ounces of white gum paste into a ¾-inch rope.

2.   Cut thirteen ¾-inch-long pieces from the rope. Roll each piece into a ball.

3.   Insert a toothpick through the center of each ball before it dries. Let the balls harden for at least a few hours or overnight.

4.   When they are dry, fill a lidded plastic container with pearl luster dust. Place the balls inside the container and close the lid tight. Shake the container to coat the balls in pearl dust. Place the pearls in a small strainer to remove excess dust.

5.   String all the pearls on a cloth-covered wire. When the cake is finished, twist the wire to form a bracelet, leaving just more than ¾ inch of space for a clasp, and affix the pearls to the cake base with a dab of Royal Icing.

6.   For the clasp, form a small oval out of gum paste, approximately ¾ inch long and ⅛ inch thick. Paint it with gold metallic luster dust and attach it with a dab of icing to the wire space between the two end pearls.

For the cake base

Dye 2 pounds of fondant pale pink. Roll it out to ⅛ inch thick and cover the cake base.

MAKE AND ASSEMBLE THE CAKE

1.   Prepare the cake batter and bake in 3 half-sheet pans as directed in the recipe. Let it cool for 20 minutes, remove from pans, then wrap tightly in plastic wrap and freeze for at least one hour. (This makes the cake easier to cut.)

2.   While the cake is chilling, make the frosting and Royal Icing.

3.   Cut six 11 x 7-inch rectangles of cake. Place a dab of filling on the larger rounded-edge, rectangular cake board and place the first layer of cake on top. Top the cake with ½ inch of filling, add the middle cake square, top that with ½ inch of filling, and place the third cake square on top. When the top layer of cake is on, push down slightly to secure the layers.

4.   Cut 3 dowels to the height of the bottom tier, and insert one in the center and one toward each corner, staying at least 1 inch in from the outer edge of the cake.

5.   Spread the doweled area with a thin layer of filling. Place the smaller rectangular cake board (with rounded edges) on top of the bottom tier. Spread it with a thin layer of filling then build the second tier from three layers of cake, filled with ½-inch layers of filling. When the top layer of cake is on, press down slightly to secure the layers.

6.   Now you have a block of cake to carve. Begin curving the edges by trimming with a serrated knife, and sculpt the cake into a handbag shape like the one pictured here. If the cake is

shifting while you try to trim, freeze it for at least an hour before cutting. Cut away any cardboard that is showing with a serrated knife or scissors. When you are done sculpting, the cake should be approximately 10½ x 6½ inches at the bottom and 8½ x 3 inches at the top. The total height of the cake should be about 8 inches.

7. Crumb coat the outside of the cake with a very thin layer of filling.

8. On a plastic mat covered with cornstarch, roll out the chocolate fondant to ¼ inch thick and cover the entire cake. Trim off the excess and save it for the flap. Use a stitching tool or toothpick to create stitch marks where the seams of the bag would be found on the sides.

To make the flap:

9. Roll out the remaining chocolate fondant to a 10 x 10 inch square, ⅛ inch thick. Follow the template to create the flap. Roll the fondant up loosely like a jellyroll then dampen the flap area on the cake with a moistened brush. Place the flap directly onto the cake, making sure the rounded edges hang down. Once the flap is on use a paring knife or X-acto to cut the excess fondant off the flap and make it fit perfectly on the cake. The flap extends 3 inches onto the back of the cake. (See the illustration.)

10. To decorate the edge of the flap with trim, roll out the reserved caramel gum paste into a long strip, approximately 22 inches long by ½ inch wide and ⅛ inch thick. Moisten the edge of the flap with water. Roll up the strip to make it easier to handle. Starting at the back of the flap, attach the gum paste and slowly unroll it all along the edge of the flap,

following the flap's edge. Once it is on, adjust to make it straight and use a stitching tool or toothpick to make stitch marks along both edges of the trim. (See detail shot.)

11. Use icing to glue the cake onto the center of the cake base. Let it set for a few minutes.

12. Attach the handle to the center of the handbag flap with icing. You may need to hold it in place for a few minutes until the icing has dried. If the handle does not feel secure, you may need to scrape off the old icing and reapply. It is okay if a little extra oozes out the side. You can remove it with a toothpick once the handle is attached.

13. Next attach the rings of the handle. Use the top of a #4 pastry tip to create holes in the cake on either side of the handle loops. Place icing on both ends of the ring pieces and insert one end into the cake and the other into the loop of the handle. Repeat this method for the remaining 3 pieces.

14. Dye a small amount of the Royal Icing pale blue and use it to attach the bow to the lower edge of the flap, and attach the flowers in a random pattern onto the lower right side of the front of the cake. Pipe dots of pale blue icing into the centers of the flowers.

15. Use white glue to attach a decorative ribbon around the cake base.

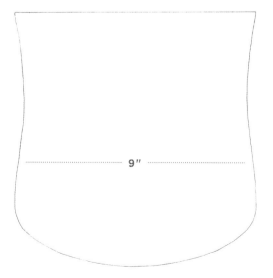

9"

What You Need

CAKE

2 cake recipes
(see *Basic Recipes* pages 49–52)

2 filling recipes
(See *Basic Recipes* pages 55–57)

1 recipe Royal Icing (page 58)

MATERIALS

8½ pounds of fondant (store-bought or page 60)

Cornstarch (for rolling out fondant)

Food-coloring gels: egg yellow, buckeye brown, super red, leaf green, navy blue

Shortening (for rolling out gum paste and fondant pieces)

Vodka (for wood-staining technique)

1 pound gum paste

EQUIPMENT

Toothpicks

One 14 x 18-inch cake base (made from three pieces of foam core or store bought)

Large rolling pin

Strainer

Dry pastry brush

Fondant smoothers

Paring knife or X-acto knife

Medium paintbrush with stiff bristles

Two 5 x 12-inch cardboards or foam core, glued together (this will be the base for the wine crate)

1 foam core board cut in a wine bottle shape (see template, page 205)

Ruler

Small serrated knife

Small offset spatula

3 wooden or plastic dowels

Plastic mat

Small rolling pin

1½-inch round cutter

Large soft paintbrush

Scissors

Food markers (optional)

Decorative ribbon

White glue

TECHNIQUES

Dyeing fondant and gum paste (page 40)

Wood staining (page 42)

Covering cake base with fondant (page 36)

Filling cake (page 31)

Crumb coating cake (page 33)

Covering cake in fondant (page 34)

Piecing fondant (page 36)

Doweling cakes (page 37)

Deconstructing sculpted cakes (page 38)

Measuring gum paste and fondant (page 61)

Wine Bottle Cake

YIELD: 30 TO 35 SERVINGS

We have made this cake for the birthdays of many wine connoisseurs. Everything is edible, even the straw in the crate. The guests are always so surprised to find out this is a cake! Personalize the cake by decorating the label with the name of the person you're celebrating with and his or her special date.

Method

MAKE THE DECORATIONS

Cake Base

1.   Dye 1 pound of fondant light brown. Using the brown fondant and 2 pounds of white fondant, follow the directions on page 42 for the wood-staining technique. Roll out the brown and white fondant to slightly thicker than ⅛ inch, cover the cake base with it.

2.   Use a ruler and a paring knife to mark off seven 2-inch intervals. Cut all the way through the fondant, to create 7 rows. Divide the panels into what look like wooden floor panels by marking off in random intervals. Imagine that each piece of wood is approximately 2 inches wide by 9 inches long, and that they start and end at different places (see photo).

3.   Once you have all the panels indented, stain your board with a mixture of ½ teaspoon brown food-coloring gel and ½ cup vodka. For an extra detail, use a toothpick and make holes at the ends of each wood piece to look like nail holes.

MAKE AND ASSEMBLE THE CAKE

1.   Prepare the cake batter and bake in 2 half-sheet pans as directed in the recipe. Let it cool for 20 minutes, remove from pans, then wrap tightly in plastic wrap and freeze for at least one hour. (This will make the cake easier to cut.)

2.   While the cake is chilling, make the frosting and Royal Icing.

3.   Cut out three 5 x 12-inch rectangles, and two 11 x 3½-inch rectangles of cake (the latter are for the wine bottle). You will need to piece together some of the layers from smaller pieces of cake.

4.   For the wine crate: place a dab of filling on the rectangular cake board and place a 5 x 12-inch layer of cake on top. Top the cake with ½ inch of filling, add the middle cake square, top that with ½ inch of filling, and place the third cake square on top. When the top layer of cake is on, push down slightly to secure the layers.

5.   Make sure the sides of the crate are straight by trimming any overhanging cake with a serrated knife. If the cake is shifting while you try to trim, freeze it for an hour before cutting. Cut away any cardboard that is showing with a serrated knife or scissors.

6.   Using the template opposite, first carve each of two of the 11 x 3½-inch layers of cake into the shape of a wine bottle. Spread a dab of filling on the board that you cut in the shape of a wine bottle, and place a carved layer on top. Fill it with ½ inch of filling, then place and secure the second layer. Chill the cake for an hour. Carve the cake into the shape of half a wine bottle lying on its side. (Once the bottle is placed in the crate it will look like an actual bottle is sticking out.) Round all the edges of the cake to form the bottle. The body of the bottle will remain 2 inches high and the neck of the bottle should slope to 1 inch high.

7.   Crumb coat the outside of both the crate and the bottle with very thin layers of filling.

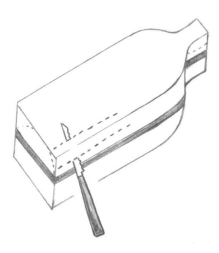

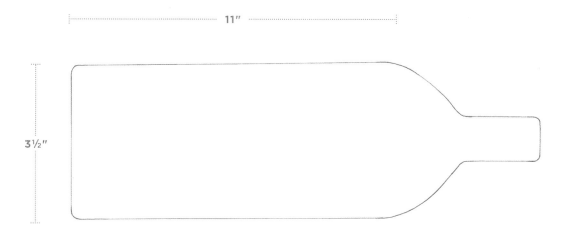

11"

3½"

8.   Dye 1 pound of fondant light brown. Twist the brown color with 3 pounds of white fondant. On a plastic mat coated with cornstarch, roll out the fondant to approximately ¼ inch thick and cut two 12½ x 6-inch pieces for the sides of the crate and two 6½ x 6-inch pieces for the ends of the crate. Place the cut pieces in the freezer for a few minutes. This will make them easier to handle and stick to the cake. Piece the fondant onto the cake. The fondant should come up about 1 to 2 inches above the edge of the cake.

9.   Dye 1½ pounds of fondant deep green. Cover the wine bottle cake with the green fondant. Create a mixture of leaf green and navy blue food coloring and vodka, and paint the entire bottle to make it dark and shiny.

10. Once the cakes are completely covered in fondant, create the wood staining effect using the brown gel and vodka. (See wood staining technique, page 42.) Paint the crate.

11. For the red top of the bottle, dye approximately 1 ounce of gum paste dark red. On a mat greased with shortening, roll it out to ¹⁄₁₆ inch. Cut out a rectangle, approximately 1¾ x 3¼ inches. Place the shorter side at the top of the bottle and wrap it around the neck. Cut another strip, 3¼ inches by ¼ inch, and wrap it around the neck at the top of the bottle. Use a 1¼-inch round cutter to cut out a circle of red gum paste and place at the top of the wine bottle. Attach it with a touch of water and smooth down the sides with your fingers.

12. For the wine label, roll out approximately 4 ounces of white gum paste to ¹⁄₁₆ inch thick and cut out a 4 x 5¼-inch rectangle. If you want to write something on the label, it is easier to do that **BEFORE** you place the label on the bottle. Use food markers or food coloring mixed with vodka to write. Place the label onto the center of the bottle just above the middle, toward the top of the bottle.

13. Use Royal Icing to glue the crate to the center of the cake base. Position the crate on a slight diagonal with your hands or fondant smoothers.

14. Cut and insert the 3 dowels in the center of the wood crate, directly underneath where you will place the wine bottle. Spread a small amount of filling to cover the doweled area and place the wine bottle cake into the crate.

15. For the "straw" packing material, take the remaining gum paste (about 10 ounces) and dye it straw yellow. Roll it into thin sheets approximately ¹⁄₁₆ inch thick and as long as you can get them. Use a paring knife to cut as many strips of straw as you can, the thinner the better. Make them all different sizes and cut until you have used all of the remaining gum paste. It is okay if the gum paste becomes dry while you are doing this. After all, real straw is very dry.

16. Use bunches of straw to fill in between the wine bottle and sides of the box. Have the straw spill over the edge in some areas to make it look realistic.

17. Use white glue to attach a decorative ribbon around the cake base.

Sushi Cake

YIELD: 20 TO 25 SERVINGS

This is one of my favorite cakes to make. We have made it for a famous sushi chef and for many sushi lovers' birthdays. It is so unexpected to bite into a piece of sushi and have it taste sweet. The best way to capture the realistic details that make this cake so great is to go out and buy some cheap sushi and use it as a model. Note that this cake is very elaborate. To make it easier, pick just one type of sushi to make. Or you may want to split this up into a few days of work.

What You Need

CAKE

2 cake recipes
(see *Basic Recipes* pages 49–52)

1 filling recipe
(see *Basic Recipes* pages 55–57)

½ recipe Royal Icing (page 58)

MATERIALS

2 pounds gum paste

Food-coloring gels: sunset orange, bakers rose, buckeye brown, super red, leaf green, lemon yellow, coal black, navy blue

Powdered food coloring: red, green

Pearl luster dust

Vodka (for painting)

Vanilla extract (for the soy sauce)

Shortening (for rolling out gum paste)

6 pounds fondant (store-bought or page 60)

Cornstarch (for rolling out fondant)

EQUIPMENT

Toothpicks

Plastic mat

Small rolling pin

1½-inch and 3-inch round cookie cutters

Cup

Palette knife

One 14 x 18-inch cake base (made from three pieces of foam core or store bought)

Large rolling pin

Strainer

Dry pastry brush

Fondant smoothers

Ruler

Paring knife or X-acto knife

Pencil

Small soft paintbrushes

Cotton swabs

Two 6 x 2-inch cardboards or foam core

Two 6 x 12-inch cardboards or foam core, glued together

Small serrated knife

Small offset spatula

Medium paintbrush with stiff bristles

4 wooden dowels

Scissors

Decorative ribbon

White glue

TECHNIQUES

Dyeing fondant and gum paste (page 40)

Covering cake base with fondant (page 36)

Filling cake (page 31)

Sculpting cake (page 32)

Crumb coating cake (page 33)

Covering cake with fondant (page 34)

Wood staining (page 42)

Doweling cakes (page 37)

Deconstructing sculpted cakes (page 38)

Measuring gum paste and fondant (page 61)

Method

AT LEAST 2 DAYS AND UP TO A WEEK IN ADVANCE: MAKE THE DECORATIONS

These decorative elements are optional — choose the ones you like best.

Soy Sauce Dish

1. Color 2 ounces of white gum paste pale blue using a touch of navy food coloring.

2. On a greased plastic mat, roll out the gum paste to ⅛ inch thick. Use the 3-inch round cutter to cut out a circle.

3. Coat the outside of a cup with shortening. Press the circle onto the bottom of the cup and let it dry for 2 days.

4. Remove the dish with a palette knife, turn it over, and paint the rim with a mixture of vodka and navy blue gel to add a decorative touch.

Chopsticks

1. On a plastic mat greased with shortening, roll approximately 2 ounces of white gum paste out to ¼ inch thick.

2. Using the small rolling pin, start at one end, gradually roll the gum paste until it is ¼ inch thick on one end and ⅛ inch thick at the other, to create the gradual slope of actual chopsticks.

3. Use a paring knife and ruler to cut out the chopsticks. They should be 8¼ inches long.

4. Make sure the chopsticks are resting completely straight and let them dry

until they are hard to the touch. Use a mixture of brown gel and vodka to stain them a light wood shade. (See wood staining, page 42.)

Cake Base

1.   On a plastic mat coated with cornstarch, roll out 3 pounds of white fondant to about ⅛ inch thick. Cover the cake base with fondant.

2.   Here we painted the fondant to look similar to a Japanese textile. To do this, take a ruler and a pencil and create a grid on a diagonal. Each square should be 1½ x 1½ inch.

3.   Use a medium paintbrush to mix navy blue gel and vodka, and paint over the pencil. At the place where each square intersects, create a curve using the tip of the brush. The painted lines should be about ¼ inch thick.

4.   Once you have the grid painted, use the tip of a cotton swab dipped in the navy paint mixture to create a dot in the center of each square. Set the base aside to dry for at least a few hours before stacking the cakes on top.

1.   Prepare the cake batter and bake in 2 half-sheet pans as directed in the recipe. Let it cool for 20 minutes, remove from pans, then wrap tightly in plastic wrap and freeze for at least one hour. (This will make the cake easier to cut.)

2.   While the cake is chilling, make the frosting and Royal Icing.

3.   Cut the cake into two 12 x 6-inch layers for the table and four 6 x 2-inch layers for the legs. Any remaining cake will be used for the sushi pieces.

4.   For the table, place a dab of filling on the 12-inch rectangle cake board and place a 12 x 6-inch piece on top. Fill cake with ½ inch of filling and place the second layer of cake on top. Push down slightly to secure the layers. The table should be about 2 inches high. For the legs, repeat the same process twice using 6 x 2-inch cake layers and one cake board for each leg. The legs should be approximately 2 inches high.

5.   Square up all edges by trimming with a serrated knife. If the cake is shifting while you try to trim, freeze it for an hour before cutting. Cut away any cardboard that is showing with a serrated knife or scissors.

6.   Crumb coat the outside of the cakes with a very thin layer of filling.

7.   Color 1 pound of the fondant light brown and twist it with the remaining 2 pounds of white fondant to prepare it for wood staining (page 42). Roll out the fondant to approximately ¼ inch thick and cover the sushi table. Be especially careful when trimming the edges because any extra fondant will show once you attach the table to the legs. Re-roll the fondant mixture and cover the two legs.

8.   Create the wood-stain effect using a mixture of brown gel and vodka. Paint the sides of each leg and the top and sides of the table to look like wood.

9.   Attach the two legs, 5¾ inches apart, to the center of the cake base, using Royal Icing as glue. Cut the 4 dowels to size, and insert 2 dowels in each leg,

evenly spaced, toward the center. Spread some icing on top over the dowels on each leg and attach the sushi table on top. Center the table on top of the legs.

Feel free to mix and match or even come up with your own. After you make the sushi pieces, proceed to steps 10 through 12.

10.   To assemble the cake: once all the pieces are complete, arrange them on top of the table. Use a dab small of icing to attach each piece to the table.

11.   Attach the chopsticks and soy sauce dish on the base in front of the sushi table. Pour about 1 to 2 tablespoons of vanilla extract into the dish for the soy sauce.

12.   Use white glue to attach a decorative ribbon around the cake base.

California Roll

1.   Using a round cutter cut out six 1½-inch rounds of cake, approximately 1 inch high. Crumb coat them with a very thin layer of filling.

2.   Color 4 ounces of gum paste with a touch of green food-coloring gel and a lot of black to form the color of seaweed wrappers. On a mat greased with shortening, roll it out to 1/16 inch thick. Cut out six rectangles, 1½ x 5½ inches. Wrap each strip around the outside of the cakes, sealing with water and leaving a hollow center to fill with the avocado, crab, and cucumber. For each piece you need one piece of avocado,

one piece of crab, and about 20 strips of cucumber.

3. **Avocado.** Dye 2 ounces of gum paste a light greenish yellow color. Roll it out to ½ inch thick and form 6 pieces about 1 inch long, ½ inch wide on one end and ⅜ inch wide at the other end. Dust the wider end with green food powder.

4. **Crab.** Roll 1 ounce of white gum paste into a rope about ½ inch thick. Cut into six ½-inch cylinder pieces. Score one end of the rounded cylinder to look like a crabstick. Paint alternating stripes with orange gel.

5. **Cucumber strips.** Roll out 2 ounces of white gum paste to ⅛ inch thick. Cut it into 120 thin strips, ½ inch long and ⅛ inch wide. Dust one side with green food powder.

6. To assemble, place one piece of crab and one piece of avocado inside the seaweed wrapper, on top of the cake. Fill in the extra space with bunches of cucumber strips.

Tuna

1. Cut out one rectangular piece of cake, 3 x 1½ inches, and trim the edges to form an oval shape. Crumb coat them with a very thin layer of filling.

2. To form the shredded daikon, roll out about 2 ounces of white gum paste paper-thin and cut as many 5 x ¹⁄₁₆ inch strips as you can.

3. Adhere the shredded pieces to the cake piece. You want enough daikon to hide the cake completely. Trim the edges as needed.

4. Dye 2 ounces of gum paste deep pink. Roll it out to form a slab of fish, about 4 inches long, 1¼ inches wide and ¾ inch thick. About 1 inch from each end, thin the piece out to ¼ inch thick and then trim back the length to 4½ inches. You can stretch and pull the gum paste to form the tuna into an irregular shape.

5. Use a paring knife to cut diagonal slits to give the look of real fish flesh. Paint the top of the tuna with pearl luster dust.

6. Attach the piece of fish on top of the daikon with Royal Icing.

Salmon

Follow same directions as for the tuna, except in step 4, dye the gum paste orange instead of pink. In step 5, use pearl dust mixed with a touch of orange gel to paint the fish.

Shrimp

1. Cut out one rectangular piece of cake, 3 x 1½ inches, and trim the edges to form an oval shape. Crumb coat them with a very thin layer of filling.

2. Make the rice. Form about 2 ounces of white gum paste into a long, skinny rope, about ⅛ inch wide. Cut the rope into small pieces about ⅛ inch wide and roll each piece to form a piece of sushi rice. Each piece of rice should be about ¼ inch by ⅛ inch. You will need as many pieces as you can make.

3. Attach the rice all over the piece of cake. Don't worry if some pieces fall off — try to get as many pieces to stick as you can. You can fill in any open spaces later with icing.

4. For the shrimp, take 2 ounces of white gum paste and roll it out to about ⅝ inch thick, 4 inches long, and 1 inch wide. Round one end of the piece and shape the other end into the tail. From the rounded side to the tail side, the shrimp's body thickness declines. Roll the tail fins paper-thin and extend them from the body about 1 inch. Use your paring knife to split the tail into two separate fins, creating little lines in each fin to give it texture. Where the body ends and the tail begins, pinch the gum paste slightly.

5. With a paring knife, make one line down the center of the shrimp. Form horizontal lines, about ½ inch apart all the way down the shrimp's back.

6. Paint the shrimp's tail dark orange with a mixture of orange and red gel. Paint the rest of the shrimp's back with horizontal lines, being careful not to paint the entire shrimp solid orange.

7. Attach the shrimp to the top of the cake covered in rice with a small amount of icing. Roll out a paper-thin strip of seaweed, using the extra gum paste from the seaweed of the California Rolls, about ½ inch wide, and wrap it around the shrimp and cake. If it is not sticking on its own then attach it with a dab of water.

Wasabi

1. Dye ½ ounce of gum paste lime green.

2. Use your fingers to bunch the gum paste together, pulling and pushing to form the realistic and dry paste look of wasabi.

Ginger

1. Dye ½ ounce of gum paste pale pink.

2. Roll it out as thin as you can, as thin as paper if possible, and cut out as many round shapes as you can. They should not be perfect circles — the more irregular, the better.

3. Take all the pieces and pinch them into a ball similar to a small dumpling, about 1½ inches wide and 1 inch tall.

4. Fold back the edges of the gum paste and dust just the outside edges with a hint of red food powder, using a small paintbrush.

Sugar Stiletto and Shoebox Cake

YIELD: 25 TO 30 SERVINGS

This is one of our best-known cakes at Confetti Cakes. People have dropped off their actual shoes and sent digital pictures for us to replicate in sugar. The shoebox and lid are made entirely out of cake and filling. The tissue paper and shoe are made from gum paste so everything is entirely edible. Most of the women we have made this cake for have saved their shoes in airtight plastic containers as a keepsake!

This cake is all about the stiletto, and the gum paste is what gives it the structure to stand on its own. Do not substitute fondant when making the shoe. You will need the gum paste to ensure that everything will dry properly, remain sturdy, and not crack. If you are having a problem with humidity, start the decorations even sooner.

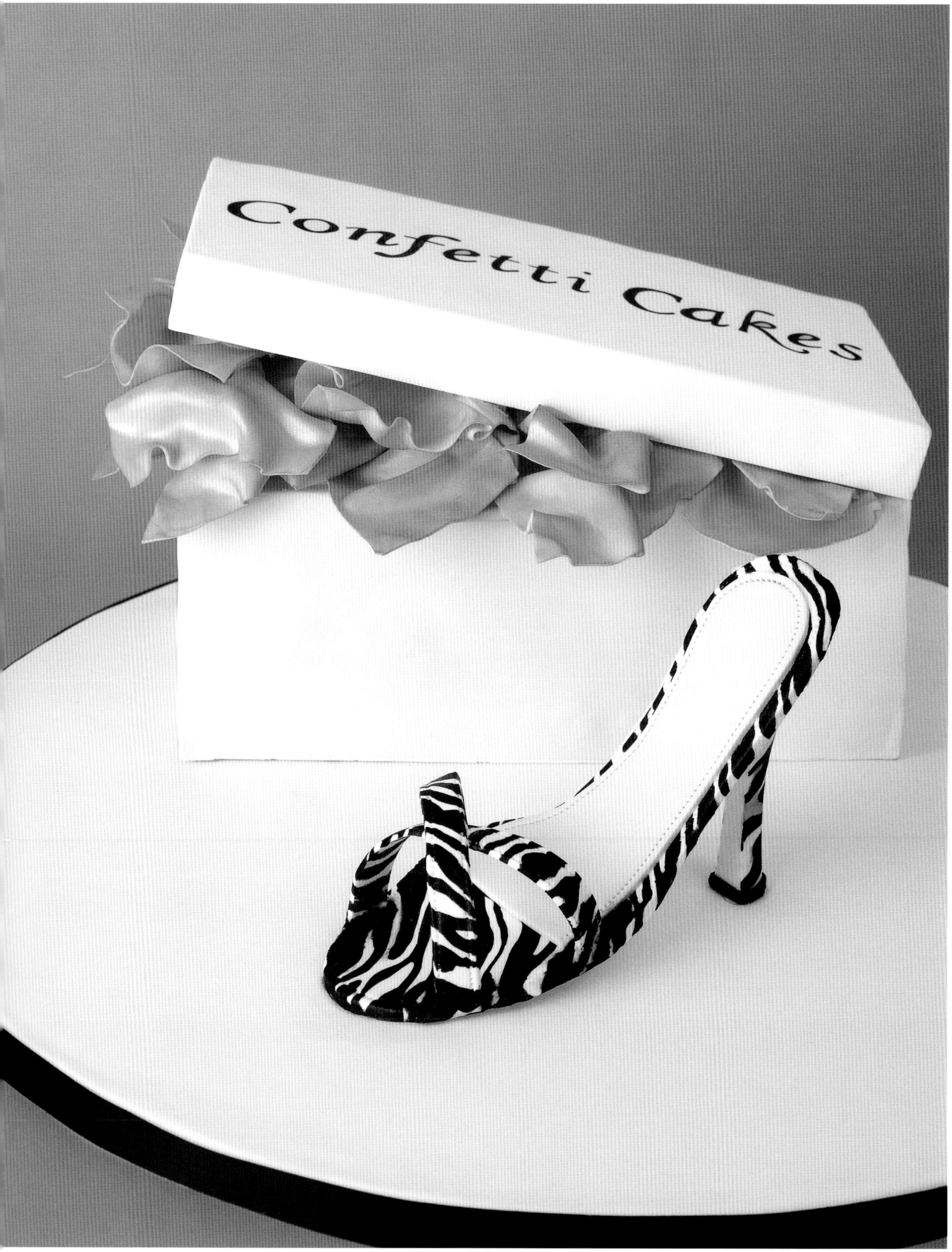
Confetti Cakes

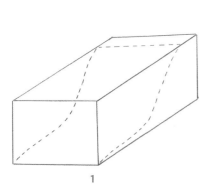

1

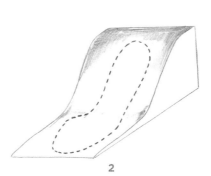

2

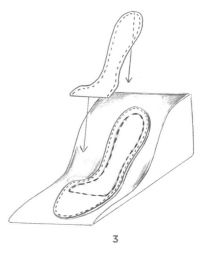

3

What You Need

CAKE

2 cake recipes
(see *Basic Recipes* pages 49–52)

1 frosting recipe
(see *Basic Recipes* pages 55–57)

1 recipe Royal Icing (page 58)

MATERIALS

1½ pounds gum paste

Shortening (for rolling out gum paste)

Lemon extract

Vodka

Pearl luster dust

Watermelon petal dust

Food-coloring gels: rose pink, coal black, buckeye brown

8 pounds fondant
(store-bought or page 60)

Cornstarch (for rolling out fondant)

EQUIPMENT

Block of Styrofoam,
9(l) x 4(w) x 4(h) inch

Small serrated knife

Parchment

Scissors

Plastic mat

Small rolling pin

Ruler

Paring knife or X-acto knife

Stitching tool (optional)

Toothpicks

Plastic wrap

One 18-inch round cake base
(made from three pieces of foam core or store-bought)

Large rolling pin

Strainer

Dry pastry brush

Fondant smoothers

Small offset spatula

Four 5½ x 11-inch foam core boards, cut in advance for the bottom of shoebox and the lid, two glued together for each

1 wooden dowel, approximately 7 inches long

Pastry bag and coupler

Pastry tips: #2, #4

Large paintbrush

Small paintbrush

Decorative ribbon

White glue

TECHNIQUES

Dyeing fondant and gum paste (page 40)

Covering cake base in fondant (page 36)

Filling cake (page 31)

Crumb coating cake (page 33)

Covering cake in fondant (page 34)

Filling a pastry bag (page 38)

Doweling cakes (page 33)

Deconstructing sculpted cakes (page 38)

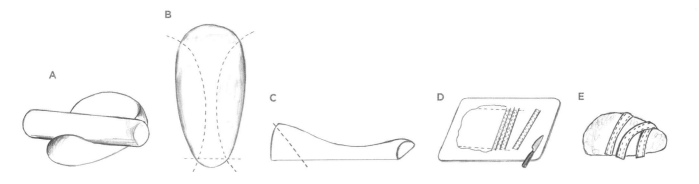

A   B   C   D   E

Method

DECORATIONS

AT LEAST 1 WEEK IN ADVANCE: MAKE THE SHOE

1. **To make the sole:** Cut a piece of Styrofoam into an elongated triangle and give it the shape of an actual stiletto's arch (diagram 1). Place a piece of parchment on the Styrofoam mold for the gum paste to rest on.

2. Use the template on page 217 as a guide to form the shape of the sole. On a plastic mat greased with shortening, roll out approximately 4 ounces of white gum paste to ⅛ inch thick. Cut out the shape of the sole. Use the stitching tool or a toothpick to create stitch marks around the border. Place the sole on the center of the Styrofoam mold (diagram 2) and let dry for at least 1 week.

3. **To make the heel:** Roll approximately 2 ounces of white gum paste into a ball. With a small rolling pin, starting ⅓ of the way in from the edge, roll the gum paste to approximately ½ inch thick (diagram A).

4. Follow the template on page 217 to create the sides of the heel (diagram B). Use your fingers coated in shortening to round out the sides of the heel and cut off the bottom end so it becomes flat. The top of the heel should be sloped at a 45-degree angle (diagram C). Let the heel dry for 1 week.

5. **To make the straps:** Roll a ball of plastic wrap into the shape of the front of a shoe. This will be used as the mold to hold the straps while they dry. If you prefer a larger arc, just use a glass turned on its side.

6. Create straps of varying lengths and widths (diagram D). For the zebra shoe, we made 2 straps from white gum paste rolled to ⅛ inch thick and cut 5 inches long and ½ inch wide. Before it was shaped we used the stitching tool (or the end of a toothpick) to create stitch marks along each edge. The straps are fragile, so make a few extra as back-ups in case of breakage.

7. Lay the straps over the plastic wrap or a drinking glass to dry for 1 week (diagram E).

AT LEAST 2 DAYS IN ADVANCE: MAKE THE TISSUE PAPER

1. Dye 1 pound of gum paste pale pink. On a plastic mat greased with shortening, roll out large sheets of gum paste as thin as you can without tearing. Using a sharp knife, cut 20 to 25 pieces of tissue paper not larger than 4-inch squares. Keep re-rolling the gum paste until it is used up. The more you vary the size, the more realistic it will look. Let the squares dry resting on crumpled pieces of tissue paper on a tray for at least two days and up to one week.

Cake Base
Dye about 3 pounds of fondant pale pink. Roll it out to ⅛ inch thick and cover the cake base.

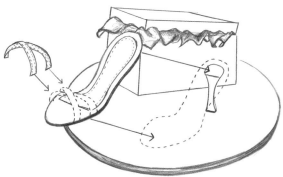

MAKE AND ASSEMBLE THE CAKE

1.   Prepare the cake batter and bake in 2 half-sheet pans as directed in the recipe. Let it cool for 20 minutes, remove from pans, then wrap tightly in plastic wrap and freeze for at least one hour. (This will make the cake easier to cut.)

2.   While the cake is chilling, make the frosting and Royal Icing.

3.   Cut out four 5½ x 11-inch rectangles of cake.

4.   Place a dab of filling on a rectangular cake board and attach one layer of cake. Top the cake with ½ inch of filling, add the middle cake square, top that with ½ inch of filling, and place the third cake square on top. When the top layer of cake is on, push down slightly to secure the layers. Place the last cake square (for the lid) on a cake board.

5.   Now you have two separate cakes, one about 4½ inches high for the shoebox and the other about 1 inch high for the lid. Trim to square up all the edges of both cakes with a serrated knife. If the cakes are shifting while you try to trim, freeze them for an hour. Cut away any cardboard that is showing with the serrated knife or scissors.

6.   Crumb coat the cakes with a very thin layer of filling.

7.   On a surface coated with cornstarch, roll out 5 pounds of white fondant to ¼ inch thick. Cover the box and the lid with fondant, paying careful attention when cutting away the excess. You want completely straight edges on both cakes.

8.   Attach the shoebox to the cake board with Royal Icing, leaving ample room for the shoe on the other side.

9.   Insert the dowel into the cake 2 inches in from the front of the box in the center. It should stick out at least 1 inch above the cake.

10. To attach the lid of the shoebox, create a line of icing along the top of the back of the box and the top of the dowel. Rest one edge of the lid against the back of the cake, and the other on top of the dowel. The lid should be at an incline. Allow 10 minutes for the icing to set.

11. Before attaching the tissue paper, dust the edges with a mixture of pearl luster dust and watermelon petal powder with a dry brush. The dust tends to float into the air, so work away from the cake when dusting.

12. With stiff icing in a pastry bag fitted with a #4 tip, attach the pieces of tissue paper. Place the pieces of paper in between the box and the lid one at a time. Fill in the entire area so you cannot see through to the other side.

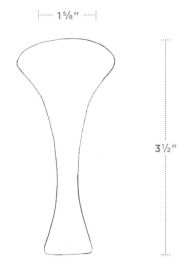

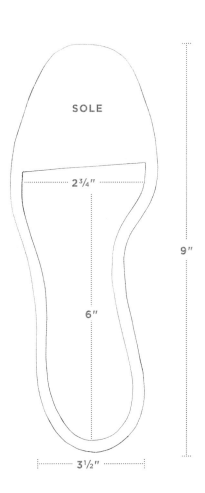

13. Assemble the shoe. Dye a tiny amount of gum paste (about the size of a pea) black and roll it out to ¹/₁₆ inch thick. Cut out and attach the thin strip of black gum paste to the heel with a dab of water (see photo). Let it dry for 10 minutes.

14. Color 2 ounces of gum paste flesh color. Roll it out to approximately ¹/₁₆ inch thick and use the template (page 217) to cut out the inner sole of the shoe. Attach it to the hardened sole (while it's still on the shoe mold) with a touch of water. Add stitching details around the edge, if desired (diagram 3).

15. Paint the heel, sole, and straps of the shoe using a mixture of black gel and vodka, in the zebra pattern. Let the paint dry for about 10 minutes.

16. Use the icing and a #2 tip to glue the heel onto the board. Turn the hardened sole of the shoe over and place dots of icing at the front (toe) and back (heel). Attach the sole of the shoe to both the standing heel and the board using the icing. With the icing, attach the two straps in a crisscross pattern. Place one strap first, attaching it to the front of the shoe on an angle. Wait a few moments for it to dry and then attach the second strap using the same method.

17. Use white glue to attach a decorative ribbon around the cake base.

Resources

CONVERSION TABLES

LIQUID CONVERSIONS
3 teaspoons = 1 tablespoon
1 tablespoon = ¼ ounce
4 tablespoons = 1 ounce
¼ cup = 2 ounces
⅓ cup = 2¾ ounces
½ cup = 4 ounces
¾ cup = 6 ounces
1 cup = 8 ounces
16 tablespoons = 1 cup
2 cups = 1 pint
1 pint = 16 ounces
2 pints = 1 quart
1 quart = 32 ounces

WEIGHT CONVERSIONS
4 ounces = ¼ pound
8 ounces = ½ pound
12 ounces = ¾ pound
16 ounces = 1 pound
20 ounces = 1¼ pounds
24 ounces = 1½ pounds
28 ounces = 1¾ pounds
32 ounces = 2 pounds

Acknowledgments

THIS BOOK IS THE WORK OF SO MANY AMAZING PEOPLE. MY UNENDING GRATITUDE GOES TO:

Stacey Glick, my fantastic agent, who helped me navigate the literary world and found us a fabulous home with Little, Brown.

Christie Matheson, my partner through this enormous project, who listened to my every concern and shared the same sense of style throughout. Her inventive mind took the most complicated directions and simplified them so anyone can make our magical cakes and cookies.

Karyn Gerhard, my magnificent editor, who I swear is Wonder Woman in disguise. Her creative ideas and unending knowledge of baking and books, not to mention patience and guidance through the entire process, were outstanding. Her consistent support and efficiency are an amazing combination—she wears all her hats so well!

Alexandra Rowley, the fabulous photographer, who brought so much more to this project than just her incredible eye and whose style and patience have made this book everything we wanted.

Gary Tooth, our fantastic design wizard, who is one of the most ingenious people I have had the pleasure to work with. Thank you for listening to every concern and coming up consistently with creative solutions.

The staff at Little, Brown, including Jill Cohen for her enthusiasm and for believing that the world should have access to Confetti Cakes; Denise LaCongo, our fantastic production manager; Tracy Behar, our fabulous relief pitcher; and Heather Fain, our tireless publicist at Little, Brown.

Two people who were invaluable to me while writing this book: Risa Kessler, my very own guardian angel, whose brilliant mind and depths of knowledge have helped to make this book what I wanted; and Kate Sullivan, my friend and custom cake maven, who lent tremendous amount of advice and encouragement through the entire book-writing process.

SPECIAL THANKS GO TO THE PEOPLE IN THE BAKERY:

Mark Randazzo (a.k.a. "Mark in the bakery"), who makes coming to work every day a pleasure. His incredible talent, impeccable organization, and tremendous assistance with everything from the techniques to the templates and illustrations were invaluable.

Candice Corbin, my wonderful assistant, whose perseverance every day makes it possible for me to get the cakes done. Her constant smile and multitasking skills have helped my heart and my company to grow.

"The girls" of the bakery. Each of them has directly and indirectly helped make this book possible: Jeri, Lori, Jill, Gail, Holly, Alexandra, and Daryl.

My lawyers, Allison Lucas and Alan Franklin, for all of their support and knowledge, and for caring a great deal about my business and me personally.

There are too many friends and family members to thank, but each one has shown incredible support and understanding. From asking what they could do to help to wondering "when is the book going to be finished?" Thank you for caring!

LOTS OF LOVE GOES TO:

My brother Eric, and Jacqueline, for your amazing computer support, your encouraging ideas, creative assistance, and so much more.

My grandpa, who taught me how to draw; my grandma, who always tells me to "give extra cake"; and my grandmomi, who first taught me how to bake. Their constant love and support are in my heart every day.

My Marc, "my betrothed." Your love, patience, and attention have carried me through and make every moment outside the bakery fun and filled with happiness. I love you.

Index